Seeking in Solitude

Princeton Theological Monograph Series
K. C. Hanson, Charles M. Collier, D. Christopher Spinks,
and Robin Parry, Series Editors

Recent volumes in the series:

Alfred H. Yuen
Barth's Theological Ontology of Holy Scripture

Andrew Shepherd
*The Gift of the Other:
Levinas, Derrida, and a Theology of Hospitality*

Mara Brecht
*Virtue in Dialogue: Belief, Religious Diversity,
and Women's Interreligious Encounter*

Dick O. Eugenio
*Communion with the Triune God:
The Trinitarian Soteriology of T. F. Torrance*

Mark R. Lindsay
*Reading Auschwitz with Barth:
The Holocaust as Problem and Promise for Barthian Theology*

Brendan Thomas Sammon
*The God Who Is Beauty: Beauty as a Divine Name
in Thomas Aquinas and Dionysius the Areopagite*

Brian C. Howell
*In the Eyes of God: A Contextual Approach
to Biblical Anthropomorphic Metaphors*

Sarah Morice-Brubaker
*The Place of the Spirit:
Toward a Trinitarian Theology of Location*

Seeking in Solitude
A Study of Select Forms of Eremitic Life and Practice

BERNADETTE McNARY-ZAK

☞PICKWICK *Publications* · Eugene, Oregon

SEEKING IN SOLITUDE
A Study of Select Forms of Eremitic Life and Practice

Princeton Theological Monograph Series 210

Copyright © 2014 Bernadette McNary-Zak. All rights reserved. Except for brief quotations in critical publications or reviews, no part of this book may be reproduced in any manner without prior written permission from the publisher. Write: Permissions, Wipf and Stock Publishers, 199 W. 8th Ave., Suite 3, Eugene, OR 97401.

"Carthusians Mark 900th Anniversary of Founder's Dies Natalis," by Cori Fugere Urban. Copyright © Vermont Catholic Tribune, October 5, 2001, pages 11–14. Reprinted in the booklet, *Silence and Solitude: Two Essays on the 900th anniversary of St. Bruno's death* by Cori Fugere Urban and Philip F. Lawler (Charterhouse of the Transfiguration, 2005). Permission granted.

Pickwick Publications
An Imprint of Wipf and Stock Publishers
199 W. 8th Ave., Suite 3
Eugene, OR 97401

www.wipfandstock.com

ISBN 13: 978-1-60608-969-9

Cataloguing-in-Publication data:

McNary-Zak, Bernadette.

    Seeking in solitude : a study of select forms of eremitic life and practice / Bernadette McNary-Zak.

    x + 150 pp. ; 23 cm. Includes bibliographical references.

    Princeton Theological Monograph Series 210

    ISBN 13: 978-1-60608-969-9

    1. Eremitic life. 2. Spiritual life—Catholic Church. 3. Asceticism. I. Title. II. Series.

BX2845 .M36 2014

Manufactured in the U.S.A.

Contents

List of Illustrations vi

Preface vii

Acknowledgments ix

1. Introduction 1
2. The Threefold Good: The Camaldolese Congregation 23
3. Remembering in Silence: The American Carthusians 43
4. Contemplation in Solitude: The Order of Cistercians of the Strict Observance 63
5. A Listening Presence: The Hermits of Bethlehem in the Heart of Jesus 81
6. Framing a Worldview in Solitude 103
7. Conclusion 127

Bibliography 139

Illustrations

Tables

Eremitic Practice in the Camaldolese Benedictine Tradition 34

Eremitic Practice in the Camaldolese Hermits of Montecorona 40

Images

Trinity of Presence and the Hermits of Bethlehem 96

Social Relationships and Eremitic Life and Practice 104

Aspects of Solitude in Eremitic Life and Practice 114

Preface

Perhaps the undeniable persistence of the transformative potential of the desert as an operative symbol in the Christian tradition and imagination is attributed to the fact that it remains suggestive of ambivalence.[1] Throughout the centuries, Christians have been drawn to dwell in desert space. In some cases, this space is designated as desert space due to its geographic features; in other cases, this space contains a range of other topographic features and is marked as desert space in a metaphoric or symbolic sense. In either case, for the Christian the desert has been, and continues to be, a site of encounter with the divine. The desert is marked as space where embodiment and knowledge, where encounter and awareness, are possible.

This book considers how some contemporary Roman Catholic hermits are framing, and dwelling in, constructed monastic and eremitic spaces in the United States. In the silent presence of their God, serving in solitude, the lives of these Roman Catholic hermits are indicative of a sustained endeavor in the Christian tradition to reside in a space defined by the potential for encounter. Through the cultivation of their eremitic practice, in forms of withdrawal from the dominant society and acts of ascetic discipline, penance, and prayer, these hermits construct the spaces in which they dwell. Symbolic language serves to shape a worldview in which physical space and personal state of being are interwoven, as one is defined in intimate relation with the other. Whether eremitic space is located on a mountain top in Vermont, in a densely wooded area in New Jersey, in the marshland of South Carolina, in the valleys of Utah, or in the wilderness of California, it is converted by the desire and potential for transformation. Ripe with potential, these spaces are laden with participation and meaning. By envisioning their lives and practices in the contexts of an established Christian worldview, biblical interpretation, and historical lineages of previous exemplars, these hermits anchor the need for, and expectations of, such space in a long tradition of recognizably

1. A Carthusian Monk, *Wound of Love*, 120.

Preface

acceptable responses. Diverse in form and expression, the lives and practices of these hermits share a heritage and historical imagination that continues to draw public attention and beg explanation. How does space function as a site of transformation for these hermits? How are they creating an environment for this state of being to be maintained in the United States? Consideration of how these select eremitic forms mark space further expands and extends the ways in which desert spirituality is being conceived in these particular contexts.

Acknowledgments

THERE ARE MANY PEOPLE WHO PROVIDED ENCOURAGEMENT AND SUPport during the research and writing of this book. I am especially grateful for the institutional and departmental support that I received from my administrative and faculty colleagues at Rhodes College. In particular, the reception of a rotating endowed chair provided sustained and necessary funding and made much of this work possible. In June 2008, after reading *Silence, Solitude, and Simplicity: A Hermit's Love Affair with a Noisy, Crowded, and Complicated World*, I was fortunate to have the opportunity to meet and talk with the book's author, Sr. Jeremy Hall, OSB. Sr. Jeremy's willingness to answer my questions about her experience with eremitic life and practice helped to shape and frame my thinking in important ways as I continued to hone the focus of this project. I am deeply thankful to her and to Sr. Gracemarie Maiers for that time. A sabbatical leave in the fall 2008 semester offered time for more research and for the development of an upper-level course on Christian monasticism that would allow me to draft and present some preliminary work. I give many thanks to those students for their invaluable feedback when this course was taught in the fall semester of 2010 and then, again, in 2013.

I am grateful for the library support that I received from Kenan Padgett of the Barret Library at Rhodes College, and especially for her assistance with interlibrary loan service. Bill Hook and Donna Smith of Vanderbilt University provided assistance and hospitality for two weeks in July 2011 while I worked at the James and Alexandra Heard Library.

There are many persons who provided me with assistance including, in some cases, information, feedback, or additional resources. I am deeply grateful to Marlene Weisenbeck, FSPA, to Fr. Robert Hale of the Camaldolese Hermitage in Big Sur, California, and to Fr. Basil of Holy Family Hermitage in Bloomingdale, Ohio. Special thanks go, as well, to the brother who served as guestmaster during my visit to the Cistercian Abbey of Our Lady of the Holy Trinity in Huntsville, Utah, and to those who introduced me to, and provided additional resources about, the

Acknowledgments

Carthusian Order and the Charterhouse of the Transfiguration in Arlington, Vermont. Finally, I am thankful to Fr. T. Kevin Corcoran of the Diocese of Paterson, New Jersey.

At various stages, parts of this book were shared with audiences at meetings of the American Academy of Religion and the Southeast Commission for the Study of Religion. I am grateful to Brian Campbell, Michael Turco, Anna Blair Solomon, Jayme Smith, and those students who continue to read with me and to think about the implications and influence of such efforts in the world today.

A final thanks to Charlie Collier, Christian Amondson, Jacob Martin, and Patrick Harrison of Wipf and Stock for their patient assistance in bringing this work to publication.

1

Introduction

> We see, therefore, that the Church has always been anxious to form the hermits into communities. Nevertheless, many preferred their independence and their solitude. They were numerous in Italy, Spain, France and Flanders in the seventeenth century. Benedict XIII and Urban VIII took measures to present the abuses likely to arise from too great independence. Since then the eremitic life has been gradually abandoned, and the attempts made to revive it in the last century have had no success.[1]

THESE WORDS, APPEARING IN THE EARLY TWENTIETH CENTURY EDITION of the *Catholic Encyclopedia*, form the conclusion to the entry titled "Hermit."[2] The entry traces the history and development of the eremitic life and practice in the Christian tradition from origins in the Eastern provinces of the Roman Empire to transmission in the Western provinces in the fourth century, to subsequent reform in the Middle Ages and decline in later centuries. The entry emphasizes throughout the need for the external, administrative regulation of eremitic life and practice, frequently undertaken by gathering hermits under a cenobitic form of practice. The entry concludes on a most somber note, suggesting that at the time of publication the eremitic life has little, if any, relevance in the Roman Catholic Church.

Reading the entry today, one is struck immediately by the changed perspective and environment for eremitic life and practice. If the entry were to be revised and updated for a contemporary audience, it would have to take into account a notably different set of contexts for the eremitic

---

1. Besse, "Hermit," 7:281.
2. Ibid.

vocation from those assumed and presented over a century ago. Specifically, in the context of the Roman Catholic Church, the entry would have to address the place of the eremitic life and practice since, at least, the middle of the twentieth century given the sizeable impact of the teachings of Vatican Council II (1962–1965) on the consecrated life in this period. The entry would also have to address the attention given to the consecrated life in a series of post-conciliar documents and the ecclesiastical significance of Canon 603 in the *Revised Code of Canon Law* (1983) which afforded canonical status to the eremitic vocation for the first time in the history of the Roman Catholic Church. A revised encyclopedia entry would certainly conclude on a more optimistic note, suggesting a slow and steady presence of the hermit and place for the eremitic life and practice throughout the world and particularly in the American Catholic Church. Far from being abandoned, eremitic life and practice remain embedded and espoused in the Church. As a result, speculation about the future development of eremitic life and practice would likely project a much more positive tone and perspective.

A Context of Reform and Renewal

The pre-conciliar decades of the mid-twentieth century were a transitional period for American Catholics. No longer defined primarily through their immigrant status, but not yet bearing an authoritative voice in the political, economic, and social spheres of American life, American Catholics were in the midst of intense internal debates over their collective place in, and relationship to, American society. Across the United States, American Catholics were engaged, in the pews of churches and in the public sphere, in significant secular and religious debates of the day. As historian David J. O'Brien observes, differences among American Catholics in this period were "no longer basically ethnic, nor were they yet doctrinal or ecclesiastical. Rather they had to do with the substance and the style of the Catholic presence in the United States."[3] As was the case in prior decades, American Catholic efforts for self-definition in the mid-twentieth century were necessarily set within prevailing norms of the dominant, non-Catholic, culture.[4] And so, as their fellow non-Catholic Americans worked to shape

---

3. O'Brien, *Renewal of American Catholicism*, 138.

4. McBrien, *Catholicism*, 1180–85, identifies several characteristics that differentiate Catholicism.

their own contributions to all spheres and strata of public life, so too, liberal and conservative American Catholics did the same. Specifically, American Catholics weighed their own levels of involvement in social matters, and their responses to modernism and to secularism, with the concomitant aims of continued assimilation with, and evangelization of, their fellow Americans.[5]

The efforts of American Catholics in these areas of public social life were necessarily impacted by emerging developments within the faith tradition itself. The dominant ecclesiology prior to Vatican Council II emphasized the institutional, juridical and hierarchical aspects of the Church. These aspects evident, for example, in the emphasis on the authority of the papal office, were replicated on the local, diocesan level through the emphasis on the authority of the episcopal office. This ecclesiology not only reflects the emphasis on papal sovereignty and infallibility issued from Vatican Council I (1869–70), but often does so at the expense of other elements and dimensions of the Church. Significant changes in theological reflection occurred in the period between these councils that would have a marked impact on the development of ecclesiology. Specifically, a more progressive strain of theology in the 1940s and 1950s sought to shift the emphasis of Vatican Council I by reconceiving a place for the laity and for the Church as the entire people of God. Furthermore, internal lay reform movements were an empowering element of religious life and practice for many Catholics. These reform movements were often directed toward devotion and prayer. Their distinct emphasis on the family, on forms of devotion to the Blessed Virgin Mary, and on the lives of the saints, provided American Catholics with opportunities for spiritual growth and development that were widely promoted in this period.[6] The seeds of liturgical reform were evident in these, and in other, initiatives that sought to increase lay participation and involvement.[7] Behind and within all of these efforts aimed at renewal, there was the growing and less visible postwar impulse, felt by some American Catholics, toward the contemplative life. As Benedictine

---

5. See Cross, *Emergence of Liberal Catholicism*, 206–24. See also Bellitto, *Renewing Christianity*, 198: "Groups like Catholic Action invited Christians to bring their faith to the workplace decades before Vatican II made that effort one of its hallmark missions."

6. See Dolan, *American Catholic Experience*.

7. Examples can be found in Bellitto, *Renewing Christianity*, 202–3. See also Dulles, *Reshaping of Catholicism*, 3, who observes that the period between the two world wars witnessed a rise in Protestant converts.

author Joel Rippinger observes, for many American Catholics, World War II and its aftermath called for a contemplative response.[8]

These pre-conciliar initiatives would contribute considerably to the decisions and documents later promulgated in Vatican Council II. For many monastic communities, in particular, the era of renewal in the Roman Catholic Church begun in the reform movements of the previous decades and fueled by Pope John XXIII at the opening of the Vatican Council II in the fall of 1962, provided an opportunity for evaluation and assessment of daily life.[9] The Council was a directive for change and it provided a context for the members of the Church to do so. As historian, Jay P. Dolan writes: "What this meant was that for the first time Catholic church leaders came to grips with the issues of modernity in a constructive manner."[10] The impact should not be underestimated. Dolan further describes the significance of this charge in these terms.

> Living in the midst of fundamental social and cultural changes and prodded by Vatican II to bring itself up to date, American Catholicism was about to pass through the most turbulent period of its short history. It was a time of both disillusionment and hope, of conflict and harmony, of crisis and growth. Though the significance of the changes still remained uncertain, one thing was clear. A new Catholicism was coming to life in the United States.[11]

The decrees and teachings of the Council marked a turning point for many monastic communities in the United States.

As historian Christopher Bellito observes, under Pope Pius XII (1939-58) and prior to Vatican Council II religious orders were called to examine anew "their founders' unique charisms and initial apostolates."[12] This effort was embedded in the documents of Vatican Council II. In their study of select teachings of Vatican II, scholars Richard R. Gaillardetz and Catherine E. Clifford demonstrate that "the renewal and reform of the church sought by the council was based on a concerted effort of *ressourcement*, of returning to the sources of the great Christian tradition in the Scriptures, in ancient Christian writings, and in the earliest sources of the Christian

---

8. Rippinger, *Benedictine Order in the United States*, 216–23.

9. See Dolan, *American Catholic Experience*, 425. See also Power, *Gifts That Differ*, 52–63.

10. Ibid., 425.

11. Ibid., 426.

12. Bellitto, *Renewing Christianity*, 198.

liturgy . . . The council's commitment to *ressourcement* was complemented by its equal commitment to renewing the life of the church-to an *aggiornamento* or updating necessary to make the church's teaching and witness accessible to contemporary men and women."[13] To these ends, Vatican Council II directed its attention to the religious life on several occasions; statements in conciliar documents highlight the place of the religious life in the body of the Church as well as in the specific task of ecclesiastical renewal. Within the major conciliar document, the Dogmatic Constitution on the Church (*Lumen Gentium*), emphasis was given to the specific way in which those who are committed to the religious life contribute to the life and universal call to holiness for all members of the Church through their specific practice of the evangelical counsels of poverty, chastity, obedience.[14] Through their particular form of practice, members of the religious life serve as both a witness and a model.[15] As *Lumen Gentium* states, "Through them Christ should be shown contemplating on the mountain, announcing God's kingdom to the multitude, healing the sick and the maimed, turning sinners to wholesome fruit, blessing children, doing good to all, and always obeying the will of the Father who sent Him."[16] Through these efforts, those with a particular commitment to the religious life contribute to the building of the

---

13. Gaillardetz and Clifford, *Keys to the Council*, 192. The Council issued sixteen documents; these documents varied in content and in juridical standing. See McBrien, *Catholicism*, 657–89. Fogarty, "North America," 327, writes that "the conciliar teaching that most immediately affected American Catholics was the constitution on liturgical renewal in 1964 and the subsequent use of vernacular languages. What had seemed so absolute and unchangeable, so timeless and ahistorical, what had previously set Catholics apart from other Americans and yet united them among themselves, now became the symbol of a Church immersed in human history and change."

14. Vatican Council II, *Lumen Gentium*, ch. 6, sec. 43: "The evangelical counsels of chastity dedicated to God, poverty, and obedience are based upon the words and example of the Lord. They were further commended by the apostles and the Fathers, and other teachers and shepherds of the Church. The counsels are a divine gift, which the Church has received from her Lord and which she ever preserves with the help of His grace. Church authority has the duty, under the inspiration of the Holy Spirit, of interpreting these evangelical counsels, of regulating their practice, and finally of establishing stable forms of living according to them. Thus it has come about that various forms of solitary and community life, as well as different religious families have grown up. Advancing the progress of their members and the welfare of the whole body of Christ, these groups have been like branches sprouting out wondrously and abundantly from a tree growing in the field of the Lord from a seed divinely planted."

15. Ibid., 5.39.

16. Ibid., 6.46.

earthly city,[17] give testimony to the Kingdom of Heaven[18] and are "devoted to the welfare of the whole Church."[19] These contributions are iterated again in another conciliar document, the Decree on the Missionary Activity of the Church (*Ad Gentes*), in which particular emphasis is further placed on the role of those living the contemplative life in the conversion of souls "by their prayers, works of penance, and sufferings."[20] Taken together, these statements in *Lumen Gentium* and in *Ad Gentes* emphasize the distinctive place and contributions of the religious life in the Church.

Renewal of the religious life was given specific focus in a third conciliar document, the Decree on the Appropriate Renewal of the Religious Life (*Perfectae Caritatis*). Here, renewal is driven by the claim that "such a life has a necessary role to play in the circumstances of the present age."[21] According to *Perfectae Caritatis*, renewal was to be guided by two operating principles. The first principle of renewal looks to the past and entails "a continuous return to the sources of all Christian life and to the original inspiration behind a given community."[22] In this way, the life of Christ, the testimony of the gospels, the founder and the rule, statutes, or constitutions of a given community become the foundation for renewal. The second principle of renewal in *Perfectae Caritatis* directs attention to the present and calls for "an adjustment of the community to the changed conditions of the times."[23] Renewal should address interior factors, such as manner of living, praying, working, and form of governance; renewal should be mindful of "the physical and psychological conditions of today's religious and also, to the extent required by the nature of each community, to the needs of the apostolate, the requirements of a given culture, the social and economic circumstances anywhere."[24] Additionally, attention was to be given to those specific charisms of the founders of these communities.[25]

17. Ibid.

18. Ibid., 4.31 and 6.44.

19. Ibid., 6.44.

20. Vatican Council II, *Ad Gentes*, 40. Such persons are also encouraged to found settlements in mission areas.

21. Vatican Council II, *Perfectae Caritatis* 1.

22. Ibid., 2.

23. Ibid. For an example, see the Olivetan Benedictines of Jonesboro, Arkansas, who have managed to locate a way of merging these goals in an effort to preserve a valuable piece of their traditional purpose and respond to a changed religious landscape. See Voth, *Green Olive Branch*.

24. Ibid., 3.

25. Ibid., 2. Gaillardetz and Clifford, *Keys to the Council*, 65, write that the council's

Introduction

The teachings in these and other documents connected to Vatican Council II affected those in monastic communities. By way of example, we might consider briefly select teachings regarding the composition and role of the laity in Vatican Council II's Dogmatic Constitution on the Church (*Lumen Gentium*) and the impact of these teachings on the local church. In his work "Towards a Theology of the Local Church," Joseph A. Komonchak writes that, "Two major theological assertions seem to govern the Council's statements about the local Church: first, that in its distinctive and constitutive principles, the Church is realized in local Churches; and, second, that it is in the distinctive social and cultural conditions of local Churches that the Church's catholicity is concretely realized."[26] The emphasis on the local church would come to have an enormous impact on theological development and expression in the post-Vatican Council II period.[27] Again, as Fr. Komonchak observes, the implications are relevant. He explains that, "The Church universal comes to be out of the mutual reception and communion of local Churches. The Church universal *is* the communion of local Churches."[28] It is well documented that the impact of an emphasis on the local church was felt across monastic communities. As Helen Rose Fuchs Ebaugh writes in her work *Women in the Vanishing Cloister: Organizational Decline in Catholic Religious Orders in the United States*, "Although many specific changes were effected in religious orders as a result of the renewal and adaptation process, these changes can be summarized as a process of dismantling the traditional cloister of the convent and substituting structures that emphasized greater identification with the laity in the Church."[29] Identification of nuns with the laity in this way challenged and eventually altered longstanding conceptions of social isolation for the members of

---

teaching on charisms "dismantled a pyramidal conception of the church in favor of a vision that saw the Spirit building up the church in service of its mission through baptismal charisms, the unique contributions of consecrated religious life, and ordained ministries."

26. Komonchak, "Towards a Theology of the Local Church," 16.

27. Power, *Gifts That Differ*, 52, writes, "As has often been repeated, the truly singular thing about the teaching of the Second Vatican Council is the self-image of the church adopted by the Constitution on the Church. The image of the People of God which prevails today has far-reaching effects on the way in which the respective missions of clerics and laity are conceived and lived. According to this way of looking at the church, it is the church as God's People which receives and bears Christ's mission and his sacrament in the world." See also Collins, *Contemplative Participation*, 9–35.

28. Komonchak, "Towards a Theology of the Local Church," 17.

29. Ebaugh, *Women in the Vanishing Cloister*, 21.

many female monastic communities. These communities responded to the mandate of the council to revise their constitutions in order to reflect this change and so sought answers to their purpose in contemporary society and in the church. As a result, Ebaugh writes, "many orders have substituted dedication to teaching and health-related work with the more nebulous goal of dedication to furthering the work of Christ in the world and/or serving the poor in society."[30] Although the same effects were not found universally, it was certainly the case that the challenge of renewal affected all communities.[31]

The documents and statements from Vatican Council II that addressed the religious life acknowledged the place and role of this calling in the Church in the past and called for those following this way of life to consider how best to move forward in the future. Following the council, several post-conciliar documents were issued to provide further guidance to specific communities and to facilitate implementation of the renewal of religious life. Under this guidance, individual communities and institutes held meetings and generated their own internal documents. One post-conciliar document, in particular, the Apostolic Letter, written Motu Proprio, on the Implementation of the Decrees Christus Dominus, Presbyterorum Ordinis and Perfectae Caritatis (*Ecclesiae Sanctae*), issued by Pope Paul VI on August 6, 1966, offered a framework for applying the teachings in various conciliar documents to the process of renewal and adaptation. Here, the Pope drew on conciliar teaching when he wrote that in the process of renewal and adaptation institutes should, among several other things, "strive for a genuine knowledge of their original spirit, so that faithfully preserving this spirit in determining their adaptations, their religious life may thus be purified of alien elements and freed from those which are obsolete."[32] Renewal and adaptation was, thus, guided in part by a return to origins and foundations, as the particular charisms of the founder and of the early forms were of importance in guiding the direction of institutes in the future.

It is telling that a return to these sources is recommended and is thereby stressed again thirty years later by Pope John Paul II in his post-synodal apostolic exhortation, Consecrated Life (*Vita Consecrata*), issued

---

30. Ibid., 78. See also Schneiders, *Religious Life in a New Millennium*.
31. See Massa, *American Catholic Revolution*, 75–102.
32. Pope Paul VI, *Ecclesiae Sanctae* 16.3.

on March 25, 1996, the Feast of the Annunciation.[33] Here, the Pope calls for "*fidelity to the founding charism* and subsequent spiritual heritage" of each institute.[34] Such persons were differentiated by their ability to listen and to respond to the call of God. "It is precisely in this fidelity to the inspiration of the founders and foundresses, an inspiration which is itself a gift of the Holy Spirit, that the essential elements of the consecrated life can be more readily discerned and more fervently put into practice."[35] As a result, the members of these institutes might be able "to propose anew the enterprising initiative, creativity and holiness of their founders and foundresses in response to the signs of the times emerging in today's world."[36] This effort is coupled by fidelity to "the rule and constitutions" of an institute as these "provide a map for the whole journey of discipleship, in accordance with a specific charism confirmed by the Church. A greater regard for the rule will not fail to offer consecrated persons a reliable criterion in their search for the appropriate forms of a witness which is capable of responding to the needs of the times without departing from an institute's initial inspiration."[37] The apparent emphasis on "signs" and "needs" of "the times" would come to serve as an important feature in the interpretation of consecrated life and practice.

The return to the founder and the early traditions, and the rule and constitutions, which are distinctive and identifying features of the orders and institutes addressed in both *Ecclesiae Sanctae* (1966) and in *Vita*

---

33. Pope John Paul II, *Vita Consecrata* 4: "In response to the desire expressed by the Ordinary General Assembly of the Synod of Bishops which met to discuss the theme 'The Consecrated Life and Its mission in the Church and in the World,' I intend to set forth in this Apostolic Exhortation the results of the Synod process and to point out to all the faithful-bishops, priests, deacons, consecrated persons and laity, and to any others who might be interested-the wondrous things which today too the Lord wishes to accomplish through the consecrated life. This Synod, coming after the ones dedicated to the lay faithful and to priests, completes the treatment of the distinctive features of the states of life willed by the Lord Jesus for his Church. Whereas the Second Vatican Council emphasized the profound reality of ecclesial communion, in which all gifts converge for the building up of the Body of Christ and for the Church's mission in the world, in recent years there has been felt the need to clarify the specific identity of the various states of life, their vocation and their particular mission in the church." For discussion of this work in the context of the life of the Pope, see Weigel, *Witness to Hope*, 783–85.

34. Ibid., 36. Emphasis mine.

35. Ibid.

36. Ibid., 37.

37. Ibid., 61. See also Council of Major Superiors of Women Religious, *Foundations of Religious Life*, 15–45; and Gerosa, *Canon Law*, 219–28.

Consecrata (1996) indicates a deep and abiding appeal to the past as sustaining and relevant in the present. In spite of very specific and differing contexts between the times of the founders and those of today both documents assert that it is the value of their contributions that is carried forward into the present. Hardly monolithic in form or practice, the act of continued interpretation of the lives and teachings of these founders is upheld as an essential element of the consecrated life in both documents and so, in the renewal of the consecrated life.

The attention given to the consecrated life in post-conciliar documents may be viewed further alongside developments in canon law. In particular, the transition from a relatively novel to a more firmly established presence for the consecrated life is, in part, the result of sustained lay and ecclesiastical support that is evident, for example, in the *Revised Code of Canon Law* (1983).[38] Recognizing that renewal within the Church might lead to the burgeoning of new forms of the eremitic life, the eremitic vocation was awarded canonical status for the first time in the Roman Catholic Church in the *Revised Code of Canon Law* (1983).[39] As a result, new forms of the eremitic life, which are included under Canon 603 in the *Revised Code of Canon Law* (1983), are currently being practiced and supported around the world, and across the United States, by individual Catholics whose commitment to the evangelical counsels is overseen by a plan of life under the approval of the local, diocesan bishop.

Over the past thirty years, since the *Revised Code of Canon Law* (1983) which marked the official place of the eremitic vocation in the specific context of the Roman Catholic Church, there has been increased interest on the part of the American public, Catholic and non-Catholic, to learn more about the eremitic way of life. Public attention ranges from print to video media and is found in denominational and nondenominational outlets.[40]

---

38. See Green, "Revised Code of Canon Law," 617–52.

39. The *Revised Code of Canon Law* (1983) was a significant contribution in the pontificate of Pope John Paul II. See Weigel, *Witness to Hope*, 445, that the pope envisioned the new Code as "a service to the Church's mission of evangelization and sanctification."

40. The issue of access should not be underestimated and it remains an important one. The fact that *Into Great Silence* (2006), about life in the Carthusian charterhouse of the Grande Chartreuse, was widely acclaimed and drew unexpected crowds of viewers across the nation raises questions about the curiosity in the monastic life and in the representation of monastic life to non-monastic audiences. A number of factors likely contribute to the reasons for increased visibility and attention to the eremitic life. While the public attention to monastic groups seeking solitude and silence may appear a contradiction, it is telling that there is evidence on the part of those interested in the eremitic

Introduction

Some of those cultivating the eremitic life, regardless of the form of their practice, have made themselves accessible to the American public. A wide range of publications serves to explain the eremitic vocation. Books published by affiliated presses share descriptions, explanations, and testimonials of the eremitic life from the perspectives of practitioners and pilgrims. Articles in denominational and in secular magazines introduce dimensions of the practice, and explore questions of its countercultural essence and sustainability on American soil. A quick search on the worldwide web yields specific information about the eremitic vocation and its many and varied forms. The release of several documentary films shown in theatres across the country in the last few years, including among others *No Greater Love*, *Trappist*, and *Into Great Silence* have supplied an insider's lens to the eremitic life. Prayer requests, as well as short visits, are permitted by some forms of eremitic life as a means of exercising hospitality.[41]

In the fifty years since the opening of Vatican Council II, the eremitic vocation has undergone what could be considered a period of institutionalization on American soil. At this point in contemporary American Catholicism the eremitic impulse has gained increasing visibility with the emergence of a multiplicity of forms and varieties of expression. Given that the sustained presence of the contemplative impulse has marked a place on the American landscape for the eremitic vocation, it is an opportune moment to identify and examine more closely some of the forms that the eremitic life is taking in the United States. The earlier contexts for renewed attention to the eremitic life in the middle of the twentieth century were marked by intense social and religious self-definition.[42] The current contexts of the eremitic life today in the twenty-first century, though certainly different in significant ways, are also shaped by

---

life and of those who live the eremitic life; that is to say, both groups participate in the visibility of this way of life. For those non-hermits interest likely encompasses an array of concerns, ranging from the counter-cultural dimension of the eremitic worldview to the practices and efforts of daily life; there are likely as many reasons for those hermits who are willing to share information about certain dimensions of their life and practice that may involve bearing witness, exercising compassion, love and prayer.

41. See France, *Hermits*, xiii: "It soon became clear that one of the ironies of the human situation is that those who have chosen to live outside society have always been eagerly sought out for advice on how to live with it. Hermits have built up great reputations not only, as might be expected, for heroic asceticism or spirituality but for insight into the ways of the world."

42. See Lekai, *Cistercians*, 208–12. See also Rippinger, *Benedictine Order in the United States*. Rippinger draws attention to the life and impact of Thomas Merton on 217ff.

processes of self-definition in an increasingly pluralistic society and faith tradition in the United States.[43] Impacted by the climate of change caused by a Church undergoing a period of concerted self-reflection over the fifty years following Vatican Council II, and a society in transition and flux many seek again to consider how best to be both Catholic and American.[44] As the American Catholic Church continues to define itself in the contexts of globalization and technological advancement that mark life in the twenty-first century, it must do so with the inclusion of the eremitic vocation. This book seeks to contribute to existing efforts to define and explain, on a small and specific scale, the state of the eremitic vocation in the American Catholic Church; it is hoped that this contribution, with its focus on the identification and explanation of some of the forms of eremitic life and practice currently in place, will give closer attention to the place of the contemplative practice in American life.

Defining the Hermit Today

It will be useful to begin with an operating definition of eremitic life and practice by referring to the typology outlined in one of the early sections of the post-synodal apostolic exhortation, Consecrated Life (*Vita Consecrata*).[45] *Vita Consecrata* characterizes the vocation of the Catholic hermit in the following terms.

> Men and women hermits, belonging to ancient orders or new Institutes, or being directly dependent on the Bishop, bear witness to the passing nature of the present age by their inward and outward separation from the world. By fasting and penance, they show that man does not live by bread alone but by the word of God (cf. Mt 4:4). Such a life "in the desert" is an invitation to their contemporaries and to the ecclesial community itself never to lose sight of the supreme vocation, which is to be always with the Lord.[46]

---

43. Numerous works address this from a variety of perspectives. See Smith, *Why Religion Matters*.

44. On the decades following the council in American Catholicism, see O'Brien, *Renewal of American Catholicism*. See also Gillis, *Roman Catholicism in America*. See also Heyer, *Prophetic & Public*, 42–47.

45. See Hardon, *Catechism on Consecrated Life*.

46. Pope John Paul II, *Vita Consecrata* 7. See the brief discussion of the impact on contemplative nun-hermits in Weisenbeck, *Vocation to Eremitic Life*, 104.

Introduction

By bearing witness, the hermit attests to a particular, Christian way of being that is open to both men and women. The eremitic life and practice assumes several possible forms.[47] These forms "bear witness" in distinct ways, and they reflect diverse interpretations of "inward and outward separation from the world."

One form of eremitic life and practice involves those individuals belonging to ancient orders who seek to live the hermit life. Such individuals can be members of cenobitic monastic communities which also offer a range of possibilities for the eremitic life. The pope's recognition and inclusion of the eremitic life of these individuals in *Vita Consecrata* is consistent with earlier definitions such as that found in earlier iterations of Canon 603 in the *Revised Code of Canon Law* (1983).[48] These individuals live in cenobitic communities, and they continue to live their monastic vows but do so with a quantitatively and qualitatively different degree of physical distance and separation from others.[49]

Eremitic life and practice also includes those in Institutes of Consecrated Life, among which are the Carthusians, Camaldolese, and Cistercians (Trappists). The eremitic life is a professed part of the religious vocation of these persons, a vocation devoted to contemplation.[50] "Professed members of these institutes live as hermits under obedience to their legitimate superiors in accord with their proper law."[51] According to *Vita Consecrata*:

> By their lives and mission, the members of these institutes imitate Christ in his prayer on the mountain, bear witness to God's lordship over history and anticipate the glory which is to come. In solitude and silence, by listening to the word of God, participating

---

47. The terms monk and hermit are not interchangeable here and so require some explanation; in this context, by monk is meant a member of a cenobitic community. A monk can become a hermit as in the case of the first form in *Vita Consecrata*, in which case s/he is both a monk and a hermit; or a monk can belong to an institute that is grounded in a balance between the eremitic and cenobitic spirit (or emphasizes the eremitic spirit over the cenobitic) and so is also designated a hermit as in the second form in *Vita Consecrata*; or one can become a hermit independent of the religious order or community as in the third form, in which case the person is a hermit and not a monk.

48. Its retention in Canon 603 extends these earlier efforts for this classification. See Coriden et al., *Code of Canon Law*, 467–68.

49. Rippinger, *Benedictine Order in the United States*, 216ff., talks about this in the context of the postwar contemplative impulse.

50. See Pope John Paul II, *Vita Consecrata* 8.18, and Vatican Council II, *Perfectae Caritatis* 7.

51. Weisenbeck, *Vocation to Eremitic Life*, 11.

in divine worship, personal asceticism, prayer, mortification and the communion of fraternal love, they direct the whole of their lives and all their activities to the contemplation of God. In this way, they offer the ecclesial community a singular testimony of the Church's love for her Lord, and they contribute, with hidden apostolic fruitfulness, to the growth of the People of God.[52]

The charisms of the founders of these institutes retain an important role in the identity and vision of eremitic life and practice.[53]

A final form of the eremitic life identified in *Vita Consecrata* addresses those hermits who are directly dependent on their local bishop. Here, the pope draws attention to the most recently instituted form of the eremitic life adopted previously in Canon 603 of the *Revised Code of Canon Law* (1983). Canon 603 recognized, for the first time, this form of the eremitic life as a distinct category of the consecrated life. Such canonical status identifies those who practice this form of the eremitic life as consecrated hermits or as diocesan hermits. The first part of Canon 603 situates the newly designated category in the context of existing categories; the canonical hermit is like the hermit who practices under the form prescribed by their institute. Like these, the canonical hermit cultivates a qualitatively distinct separation from the world, and maintains a life structured by the daily practices of silence of solitude, prayer and penance. The second part of Canon 603 highlights the differentiating features of the canonical hermit. The hermit in an institute follows the monastic vows and the commonly shared proper law of the institute under the direction of a monastic leader, the abbot or superior; the canonical hermit follows the three evangelical counsels and an individually designed plan of life under the authority of an ecclesiastical figure, the local bishop.

There is diversity of expression among canonical hermits as some live as individuals whereas others dwell in a community of hermits, adopting

---

52. Pope John Paul II, *Vita Consecrata* 8.18–19.

53. See Knowles, *From Pachomius to Ignatius*, 16, with regard to the new orders that arose in the revival of the eleventh century: "Compared with earlier renovations it had two distinct features. In common with all medieval movements it claimed to be a return to past excellence, but whereas previously the golden age had been situated in the sixth century, reformers were now seeking their models in earlier ages, and monastic reformers were demanding a return to the desert cradle of monarchism. The reform of the eleventh century was distinguished also by the spirit of the age: the new capacity of adolescent Europe to rationalize problems and organize on a wide scale was brought to bear upon the needs of the religious life, and a constitutional framework was gradually evolved that was capable of application to all kinds of vocation."

Introduction

the ancient form of the laura, namely, a small number of hermits who live in separate, solitary dwellings and convene daily or weekly for liturgical prayer.[54] Both expressions share the same element of separation, a key element of Canon 603.[55] Alongside the cenobitic monastic form, the anchoritic form practiced by the Desert Fathers, has informed the development of Christian monasticism; the distinct designation of the canonical hermit recovers this early element of monastic life in a highly intentional way. As the editors of *A Handbook on Canons 573–746* have keenly observed, with the canonical status of this form of the eremitic life, "The term 'religious' now applies to individuals with no obligation to common or community life and no relationship to an institute. Groups could use the category of associations of the faithful to have ecclesiastical identity if they wish."[56] The inclusion of this form of eremitic life would come to provide both opportunity and challenge.

In addition to the statement and identification of the various forms the eremitic life and practice assumes, the common substance of the consecrated life is emphasized in *Vita Consecrata*. "The consecrated life may experience further changes in its historical forms, but there will be no change in the substance of a choice which finds expression in a radical gift of self for love of the Lord Jesus and, in him, of every member of the human family."[57] Among all forms of the eremitic life outlined in *Vita Consecrata* is a common, shared purpose: to "bear witness to the passing nature of the present age by their inward and outward separation from the world."[58] In all forms, this is done primarily through contemplation fostered by separation and solitude.[59]

54. See Chryssavgis, "Fire and Light."

55. This reference to the anchoritic life is found in Beal et al., *New Commentary on the Code of Canon Law*, xvi-xvii.

56. See Hite et al., *Handbook on Canons*, 55.

57. Pope John Paul II, *Vita Consecrata* 3.14.

58. Pope John Paul II, *Vita Consecrata* 7.

59. Here I wish to emphasize that the subject addressed in this book is one particular group of persons addressed in *Vita Consecrata* (and only a sampling of that group). See *Vita Consecrata* 2: "We are all aware of the treasure which the gift of the consecrated life in the variety of its charisms and institutions represents for the ecclesial community. Together let us thank God for the religious orders and institutes devoted to contemplation or the works of the apostolate, for societies of apostolic life, for secular institutes and for other groups of consecrated persons, as well as for all those individuals who, in their inmost hearts, dedicate themselves to God by a special consecration." You can see here the many various groups of persons whose vocation falls under the category consecrated life. See also the welcome study by Cole and Conner, *Christian Totality*.

Seeking in Solitude

However, within such similarity, the particular features and practices within each form outlined in *Vita Consecrata* betray distinctive interpretations of this purpose and reflect a vibrant pluralism of meaning for the eremitic life. The forms of eremitic life defined in *Vita Consecrata* suggest a range of acceptable interpretations of the eremitic vocation in order to include those in a religious order who live the eremitic life while connected to a monastic community, those in an institute who live the eremitic life in accordance with their proper law, and those who profess the eremitic life and cultivate it under the direction of their plan of life and the diocesan bishop. This range allows for varying degrees of connection to, and separation from, community life and the outside world. As a result, it permits as acceptable multiple interpretations of contemplation and solitude.[60]

These forms are also differentiated in several other ways. While some follow a rule or guide that has provisions for the eremitic life and practice, others are structured for and by that life and practice. Some hermits are connected to a religious order overseen by an abbot or a prior, whereas others are overseen by the bishop and so are connected in a specific way to their local diocese and to the local church. As a result, there are different types of authority structures in place in the life of the hermit. There are, as well, varying degrees of involvement in the world among those identified in *Vita Consecrata*. Involvement ranges from a life of anonymity and hiddenness to one of service, hospitality and correspondence with others. Likewise, the eremitic life and practice is, in some cases, a temporary arrangement cultivated for a particular period of time; in other cases, it is a permanent commitment. In some cases, the monk can transition from a cenobitic to an eremitic life and practice as a development in the process of spiritual formation. The hermitage site, too, assumes a variety of structural forms that may include freestanding, unconnected structures in a configuration akin to the ancient laura, a charterhouse, or a hermitage located on the grounds of a monastery.

Such pluralism in theory and in form hearkens to the origins and early development of the eremitic life in the Christian tradition. Biblical precedent, as well as early Christian practice, is evidence for the place of eremitic life and practice. The fourth century practices of the desert monks of Egypt, Palestine and Syria, as well as later codification in the West through the creation, compilation and institution of rules of life contributed to its

---

60. This range appears to exist as a continuum in the institutional context of Roman Catholicism.

formation and remain foundational to each form of the eremitic life today. Perhaps, in recognition of this diversity, the current pluralism of forms of eremitic life and practice betrays a deep recognition of the contours of the origins and early historical development of the eremitic life in the Christian tradition and encompasses the patterns of vocation and practice, as well as the tensions surrounding the relationship of solitude to community, that are evident in the early lives of the desert fathers and mothers, as well as in those of Abba Antony, Abba Pachomius, John Cassian and St. Benedict of Nursia. The eremitic and cenobitic monastic impulses present in the early church are both preserved as foundational, and interpreted as contemporary and relevant, forms of Roman Catholic religious life.[61]

In some way, each of the forms of eremitic life identified in *Vita Consecrata* hearkens to the experience of the desert, and to those whose experiences are seminal in the desert spirituality of the Christian tradition. This includes those prophetic figures in the Hebrew Scriptures, especially Elijah, as well as Jesus Christ and later fourth century monks including Abba Antony and the Desert Fathers.[62] There are several general ways in which the eremitic life intentionally crafts a connection between contemporary practice and that of ancient predecessors. These include explicit referencing to specific teachings, and appeal to particular practices and explanation of eremitic experiences through the lens of such figures in the various organizing documents of the eremitic life, that is, in the rules, constitutions, statutes, and plans of life. In addition, there is a commitment to the form of life that these figures cultivated, as evident in common approaches and methods of scriptural interpretation as well as interpretation of the meaning of the desert as both a place and a state of being. In these ways, the eremitic life in each of its forms as defined in *Vita Consecrata* is projected as an extension of a lineage of practice going back to the earliest forms in the Christian tradition, and so is a persistent and foundational source for the eremitic life in the present and in the future. Such preservation is a hallmark of development.

---

61. Consider the insight of a Carthusian monk in *Wound of Love*, 105: "The first monks went deep into the desert with the intention of recovering the unity of a heart fixed only on God and also to struggle hand to hand with the Adversary, where Christ confronted and conquered him for the spiritual welfare of the Church."

62. See Van Wanroij, "Prophet Elijah Example."

Overview of This Book

This book examines select current forms of Roman Catholic eremitic life in the United States. The intentional construction of a historical lineage to previous forms in an explicit way in and through documents such as *Vita Consecrata* makes it possible to explore the current impulse for the eremitic practice in the United States and the development of recurring, defining features. American Catholic eremitic practice remains strictly defined by codes of separation, solitude and silence as the hermit dwells in the "desert wilderness," identified consistently as both a physical space and a state of being.[63] The finds of existing scholarship and the results of new research make it possible to ask fresh questions that may help us to address, explain, and map this religious phenomenon: How might we account for the recent growth and development of Roman Catholic eremitic forms in the United States? How are these forms defining Roman Catholic eremitic practice? Where are they being cultivated and how are they being interpreted in light of their intended and explicit claims about association to origins and earlier forms? How is the landscape of the United States being transformed into space whereby one can dwell in "the desert?" Consideration of the specific forms of eremitic life and, in particular, consideration of the relationship between where these hermits are-the space in which they dwell-and what they do-the place that they create through the life they live, will provide evidence with which to respond to these questions.

Following this introductory chapter, the next three chapters in this book present three select forms of Roman Catholic eremitic life and practice in the United States by considering hermits that belong to an ancient order or new institute.[64] The new institutes considered here are classified as Institutes of Consecrated Life in the context of the Roman Catholic Church. For members of these institutes, elements of eremitic life and practice are

---

63. While select forms of the Christian eremitic practice have received considerable attention, it has been largely in isolation. For example, historical overviews of the growth and development of specific forms, including the Carthusians and the Cistercians, are available. Furthermore, the eremitic practice has certainly been included in broader historical studies of Christian monasticism (see, e.g., Knowles, *Christian Monasticism*) as well as in more philosophically oriented discussions of the hermit ideal (see, e.g., France, *Hermits*). A study that treats these forms collectively and assesses them through the proposed methodological approach may provide another framework.

64. Pope John Paul II, *Vita Consecrata* 8, 18, and Vatican Council II, *Perfectae Caritatis* 7.

a professed part of their religious vocation, a vocation devoted to contemplation.[65] Given the fact that each form has distinctive features, each form represents a particular interpretation of eremitic life and practice.

"The Threefold Good: The Camaldolese Congregation," introduces the first of two of the institutes considered in this book that are grounded in the Benedictine tradition. The tenth century reforms of St. Romuald of Ravenna initiated a return to the eremitic life and practice. St. Romuald and his followers retained adherence to the *Rule of St. Benedict* and sought stricter application of select ascetic disciplines and separation. Solitude also featured prominently in the reforms of St. Romuald. Today, the eremitic life and practice is found among those who continue to be guided by these reforms, those belonging to the Camaldolese Congregation of the Order of St. Benedict and the Congregation of Camaldolese Hermits of Montecorona.

The next chapter, "Remembering in Silence: The American Carthusians," presents select elements of the eremitic practice that structure life in the Carthusian Order, founded by St. Bruno of Cologne in the eleventh century. Here, too, reform involved withdrawal and stricter discipline. Officially unconnected to the *Rule of St. Benedict*, life in the hermitage is a defining feature of Carthusian life and practice. Drawing, in part, on the examples of the early desert fathers of the fourth century, the Carthusian life is shaped by solitude, silence, and anonymity. A single Carthusian monastery, for men, located in Arlington, Vermont attests to the presence of the Order in the United States.

This chapter is followed by "Contemplation in Solitude: The Order of Cistercians of the Strict Observance." It treats the second new institute that is grounded in the Benedictine tradition considered in this book. Members of the Order of Cistercians of the Strict Observance, often commonly referred to as Trappists, trace their development to the reforms of Robert of Molesme and several colleagues who left their monastery to settle in Citeaux in the eleventh century. Subsequent developments over the course of centuries resulted in expansion of the Order to the United States. Today, there are over a dozen Trappist monasteries located in regions across the continental United States.

In the fifth chapter, discussion shifts to a form of Roman Catholic eremitic life and practice in the United States that resides in a non-monastic, diocesan, context. In accordance with the requirements identified in Canon

---

65. Pope John Paul II, *Vita Consecrata* 8, 18, and Vatican Council II, *Perfectae Caritatis* 7.

603 of the *Revised Code of Canon Law* (1983), the canonical or consecrated hermit shares with those hermits in a religious institute or monastic order, the practices of physical withdrawal from others for the purpose of solitude and prayer. Specifically, canonical or consecrated hermits publically profess adherence to the three evangelical counsels. Canonical or consecrated hermits are guided by a plan of life and their practice is overseen by their diocesan bishop. Through this relationship to the local episcopal authority, the canonical or consecrated hermit is connected to the local church in a distinct way.

This book presents one form of eremitic life and practice that has been established in accordance with Canon 603 of the *Revised Code of Canon Law* (1983). "A Listening Presence: The Hermits of Bethlehem in the Heart of Jesus" introduces this form by considering one expression found in the diocese of Paterson, New Jersey. The Hermits of Bethlehem in the Heart of Jesus have been canonically erected as a Laura of Consecrated Hermits of Diocesan Rite. Unlike those forms of eremitic life and practice considered in previous chapters, the Hermits of Bethlehem are not founded on a monastic reform movement; nor are they guided by a monastic rule or code. Rather, the Hermits of Bethlehem espouse a desert spirituality that is outlined in their plan of life. Hearkening directly and specifically to the desert wilderness experience of select biblical figures, and the Egyptian desert fathers and mothers of the late fourth century, the Hermits of Bethlehem adopt and adapt an ancient desert spirituality to the current day and context. Like their ancient desert Christian predecessors, the Hermits of Bethlehem incorporate the structure of the laura, whereby each individual hermit resides in a single hermitage situated near the church or chapel. The Hermits of Bethlehem propose a particular interpretation of eremitic life and practice that is centered in the hermitage and their plan of life guides and directs their focus in a trinity of presence and a life of contemplation. As was the case with their desert Christian forefathers and foremothers who exercised hospitality in a variety of forms that included spiritual guidance, so too, the Hermits of Bethlehem are a site of charity and hospitality for those in, and beyond, their diocese.

The particular forms of eremitic life and practice presented in each of these chapters in this part of the book are evidence for some of the ways religious space and place are being defined in the context of an American Catholic worldview. In each case, the convergence of religious experience, religious narrative, and religious ritual is rooted in a specific geographical

Introduction

location that, in turn, shapes interpretation and understanding: the wilderness, the mountain, the valley, the desert. Locations are characterized qualitatively; they are set apart, removed, and remote. Furthermore, they are intentionally structured. The space of the monastery, of the hermitage, and of the cell are carefully ordered and situated. In each chapter, then, some attention is given to how space and place are distinctively shaped and bounded through appeal to select sections of the respective constitutions, declarations, statutes, and rules of these institutes. Observations about space and place by those inside, as well as outside, the church are included in order to supply a fuller interpretation. For the sake of providing a comparative lens, each chapter bears a loosely similar internal structure: the chapter opens with a brief descriptive paragraph about the specific form of eremitic life and practice to be addressed; subsequent sections discuss some of the distinctive, organizing features of the eremitic life and practice with attention to origins and historical development as well as the specific rule or code of practice followed; each chapter closes with an attempt to articulate how the specific form is situated in a broader social or religious context in order to move toward a consideration of common features and elements in the final chapter.

Chapter 6, "Framing a Worldview in Solitude," moves from the particular presentation of specific forms of eremitic life and practice to a broader discussion of how the central common feature of solitude shapes the construction of space, place, and worldview that is situated specifically in the context of the Roman Catholic tradition of contemplative life. Through silence, separation, prayer, and penance, the hermit is oriented toward self, others, and world in a way that emphasizes the distinctiveness of eremitic life and practice in relation to society. To think about eremitic life and practice in these terms is not intended to suggest a strictly functionalist or reductionist interpretation of the eremitic life and practice; rather it is proposed as a potential framework for how one might think about and make some sense of the eremitic life and practice as a religious and distinctively Roman Catholic form of life and practice with simultaneous orientations to past, present, and future.

This chapter is also intended to provide the basis for a preliminary explanation of the sustained presence of eremitic life and practice in the specific context of American Catholicism presented in the final, concluding chapter of the book. The conclusion, then, seeks to offer in this context a response to the question of the place of the eremitic life and practice in

Seeking in Solitude

American Catholicism that hopes to neither mystify nor mythologize it, but rather, to attempt to understand it.

2

The Threefold Good

The Camaldolese Congregation

Prayer uttered out of the deepest longing for God, however, demands silence.[1]

AFTER DISEMBARKING FROM A TRAIN CARRYING RIDERS TO AND FROM THE downtown Berkeley metro stop, you can walk uphill for about a mile on a steep winding road before reaching a nondescript house that serves as an urban monastery, a center of study and prayer, to members of the Camaldolese Benedictine Order. The monastery sits amidst a row of houses in a residential area, removed from the bustle of the vibrant, sprawling University of California campus resting at the base of the hill. The back porch of the monastery overlooks the San Francisco Bay. Even on a cold, cloudy November day, the view from the top of the hill is breathtaking.

Camaldolese Congregations in the United States

Camaldolese monks and hermits trace their origins to the reform efforts of St. Romuald of Ravenna (c. 952–1027).[2] St. Romuald was a member of

---

1. Breck, "Prayer of the Heart," 41.

2. See Belisle, *Camaldolese Spirituality*, 8: "The Romualdian reform movement consisted not only in those houses founded, refounded, or reformed by Romuald and his associates, but also those houses that Fonte Avellana founded or reformed under Peter Damian, during the time before the canonical establishment of either the Avellanita Congregation or the Camaldolese Congregation." See also the entire first chapter, "General Introduction," in Belisle's book for a succinct and useful historical overview.

the abbey of Saint'Apollinare in Classe,[3] an Italian monastery connected to Cluny; envisioning a life of stricter discipline and adherence, St. Romuald left the monastery in order to live as a hermit. By cultivating withdrawal, solitude and silence, the reforms of St. Romuald provided a structural framework for a relationship between the cenobitic and eremitic elements of monastic life and practice. Author Peter-Damian Belisle writes that the spirituality of the Romualdian reform "combined the regulations of the *Rule of St. Benedict* with the charismatic and prophetic asceticism contained in the *Life of Antony* and desert monastic literature-the *Apophthegmata, The Lives of the Fathers,* and John Cassian's *Conferences*. The Romualdian vision wanted to organize the eremitical life by emphasizing greater silence, solitude, and fasting for its hermits and cenobites living under Benedict's *Rule*."[4] St. Romuald's vision is further, and appropriately, contextualized by both a broader, more general spirit of monastic reform in many of the monastic practices of his day as well as a specific desire for greater emphasis on the place of the eremitic form in the Christian life. It is in this regard, Belisle observes, that the distinctiveness of St. Romuald's reform appears especially clear: "Romuald was allowing hermits to live alone together, but under the Rule and obedience to a superior. Before Romuald, those hermits not living alone in the wilds were attached to an established monastery, under obedience to a superior of the cenobitical house. But Romuald accented the importance of solitude in his spirituality by placing cenobites and hermits living together under a hermit superior. Hermitages came into their own ecclesiastical standing."[5] St. Romuald's reform would serve not only to curb

---

3. See "St. Romuald," *Oxford Dictionary of the Christian Church,* 1426.

4. See Belisle, "Overview of Camaldolese History and Spirituality," 9. See also Hutchison, *Hermits of Grandmont,* 15, who situates Romuald in the context of a pattern evident throughout monastic history. Hutchison writes that: "The widespread opting-out of monks from the traditional monasteries in the eleventh century gave rise to a strange paradox which was repeated time and again. The monks who left regular communities to become solitaries invariably attracted followers and ended up by founding new monasteries which were merely stricter versions of those they had left in the first place. Hence, the eleventh century hermits are often indistinguishable from reformed religious."

5. Ibid., 10. See Louf, "Solitudo Pluralis," 22, who explains that the reform movements in the monasticism of the eleventh and twelfth centuries emphasized solitude and "a return to the desert" that gave rise "to several forms of eremitical life lived in community." With regard to monasticism in the Middle Ages, Sayre, *Solitude in Society,* 26 writes that "although solitude continues to be associated to some extent with the monk's life, the worldly and populous monasteries often are no longer solitudes in the classic sense; now the hermit's life if the true solitary one." For discussion of the types of hermits that arose and for the ways in which the eremitic life was lived in this period, see Ward,

The Threefold Good

laxity, but to recover a significant place for the eremitic life and practice.[6] The foundation at Camaldoli, in Arezzo, Italy, was the most successful of those instituted by St. Romuald, and it still thrives today. St. Romuald's call for a renewed emphasis on solitude and a central place for the eremitical life remain characteristic features of Camaldolese life and practice.[7]

Following continued growth and a sustained presence, the Camaldolese Congregation of the Order of Saint Benedict was officially and formally recognized by papal bull within a hundred years of St. Romuald's death.[8] Several centuries later, in 1520, a member of this Congregation, Don Paul Giustiniani, drafted the *Regula vitae eremiticae* in order to further preserve the emphasis on the eremitical practice and spirit of Camaldolese life.[9] The cultivation of Don Giustiniani's rule "gave rise to a new, exclusively eremitical congregation, which he named the Company of Hermits of St.

"Relationship between Hermits and Communities," 54–63. See also Phipps, "Romuald-Model Hermit," 65–77.

6. Dimier, *Stones Laid before the Lord*, 182, observes that under St. Romuald, the "hermits lived the Benedictine Rule in small cells with adjoining gardens, separated from one another without being connected by a cloister. Nearby they had a church with a small cloister, but there was no chapter house or common refectory. All these buildings together constituted the hermitage, the *Sacro Eremo*. A number of daughter houses were soon founded and the Order's constitutions were drafted in 1085 by Blessed Rudolph, fourth successor to Saint Romuald. Close to some of these hermitages were monasteries where religious lived a cenobitic life and where novices were formed for the eremitical life which they would later live in the hermitages."

7. See Matus, *Mystery of Romuald and the Five Brothers*, 20–21.

8. See Vigilucci, *Camaldoli*, 50, where he writes: "The Bull juridically constituted the Camadolese Congregation of the Order of Saint Benedict, deriving the name from Camaldoli which assumed the role of 'head and mother' of its own dependencies, as well as the hermitages and monasteries founded or reformed by St. Romuald, and those which had adopted the reform directives during the ensuing years."

9. As with other religious orders, the Camaldolese have a rich history of growth and decline, fragmentation and unification, as the social, cultural and religious contexts changed over their historical development. There are several excellent publications that recount this history. Here, I highlight only the two congregations whose presence is found in the United States. See Belisle, *Language of Silence*, 94, where he observes: "Because his reform work was such a discouragingly uphill battle and thankless task at Camaldoli where the majority were not then reform-minded, Giustiniani gradually focused his efforts on forming an eremitical group of like-minded hermits outside Camaldoli." See also Matus and Hale, "Camaldolese in Dialogue: Ecumenical and Interfaith Themes in the History of the Camaldolese Benedictines," 161–62. See also Leclercq and Giustiniani, *Camaldolese Extraordinary*.

Romuald."[10] Today this Company is called the Congregation of Camaldolese Hermits of Montecorona.[11]

Both congregations, the Camaldolese Congregation of the Order of Saint Benedict and the Congregation of Camaldolese Hermits of Montecorona, are classified juridically as clerical religious institutes because each is overseen by a superior who is also a member of the priesthood; however, the priesthood is not a requirement for membership in either congregation.[12] Whereas the Camaldolese Congregation of the Order of Saint Benedict, whose United States Hermitage is called New Camaldoli, retains both the cenobitic and eremitic forms of practice, those belonging to the Congregation of Camaldolese Hermits of Montecorona, commonly referred to as Montecorona or the Coronese Hermits, preserve only the eremitic form of practice. Within these distinctive expressions of the Camaldolese Order, each congregation has an established place for the eremitic practice. It is the distinctive expression of the eremitic practice in each congregation that will be considered in subsequent sections of this chapter.

Each congregation has eremitic foundations in the United States. In 1958, the New Camaldoli Congregation, whose motherhouse is the Hermitage at Camaldoli, Italy, made a foundation with donated land in Big Sur, California where it currently continues to thrive, develop and grow.[13] The hermits who reside on this foundation are also referred to as the Camaldolese Hermits of America. In addition to the rural hermitage for these male monastics in Big Sur, California,[14] the congregation once included

---

10. Vigilucci, *Camaldoli*, 147. See also Belisle, *Language of Silence*, 94–95. See also Camaldolese hermit, *In Praise of Hiddenness*.

11. Vigilucci, *Camaldoli*, 148. The Congregation of Camaldolese Hermits of Montecorona is not affiliated with the Benedictine federation. The Camaldolese Hermits' interpretation of Camaldolese origins maintains that St. Romuald founded Camaldoli as a hermitage with a guesthouse removed from the site, and that the later development of the guesthouse into a monastery was not originally intended.

12. See Canon 588 in the *Code of Canon Law*.

13. See Belisle, "Overview of Camaldolese History and Spirituality," 21, who observes that a cenobitic Camaldoli foundation was made in Texas prior to World War II. It was closed in 1935.

14. On this, see Matus and Frigerio, *Monastic Life of the Camaldolese Benedictines*, 19–20. See also Spencer and Fish, "Camaldolese Oblate Program," 169–82. There are several other American Camaldolese Benedictine foundations in the United States. Among these is Incarnation Monastery, the urban Camaldolese Benedictine monastery established in Berkeley, CA, in 1979 and Transfiguration Monastery, a rural monastery for female monastics in Windsor, NY, that was affiliated in 1986. There are several websites

Epiphany Monastery, a rural hermitage for male monastics in New Boston, New Hampshire, that was established in 1992.

In 1959, the Montecorona Congregation established its first foundation in the United States in McConnelsville, Ohio, called Holy Family Hermitage. In 1966, it was transferred to Bloomingdale, Ohio, in the Diocese of Steubenville. This Coronese hermitage houses a novitiate, and its motherhouse is the Sacro Eremo Tuscolano in the province of Rome.

Eremitic Practice in the New Camaldoli Congregation (OSB Cam.)

The *Rule of St. Benedict* is at the heart of Camaldolese Benedictine practice. The Camaldolese Benedictines incorporate those cenobitic and eremitic forms of practice identified as acceptable according to the *Rule of St. Benedict*.[15] In his *Rule*, St. Benedict made provisions for a range of monastic practices. Upon examination, it is clear that these provisions were grounded, in part, in a definite relationship between the cenobitic and eremitic forms of monastic life. These provisions appear in the first rule of the *Rule of St. Benedict* which addresses the four types of monks of St. Benedict's day. Here, St. Benedict provides a perspective on the cenobitic and eremitic forms of monastic life that sharply contrasts them from other forms. He differentiates the cenobitic and eremitic forms in terms of their distinct structural frameworks: the cenobitic form is located in a monastery and governed by a rule overseen by an abbot, whereas the eremitic form may emerge from the cenobitic form for those who will focus their practice in a more individual pursuit. St. Benedict then distinguishes the eremitic practice further with attention to another defining feature. Of those assuming the eremitic form, St. Benedict writes: "Self-reliant now, without the support of another, they are ready with God's help to grapple single-handed with the vices of body and mind."[16] Spiritual combat with vices thus marks a specific activity of the hermit, according to St. Benedict.

---

that include information as well. For the Hermitage, see www.contemplation.com; for Incarnation Monastery, see www.IncarnationMonastery.org.

15. For a pertinent study of Benedictine spirituality, see Stewart, *Prayer and Community*. See also Dreuille, *Seeking the Absolute Love*, 126–33, for a succinct discussion of St. Benedict and the *Rule of St. Benedict*.

16. Fry, trans., *Rule of St. Benedict*, 1.

Seeking in Solitude

The specific nature of the relationship between cenobitic and eremitic practice intended by St. Benedict in the first rule is the subject of ongoing scholarly debate. Certainly, the perspective St. Benedict gives in the first rule provides a clear acceptance of the cenobitic life as a common and accessible form of monastic practice; the fact that St. Benedict writes the remainder of his *Rule* to encourage life under the cenobitic form is evidence that its regulation, which could, to some extent, require a clear statement of its connection to other forms, was an issue he sought to address. With regard to the eremitic form, the perspective offered in the first rule appears to contain both a descriptive and an analytical orientation, and we must recall that St. Benedict, himself, spent time living as a hermit, a fact that certainly impacted his perspective. Taken literally, St. Benedict's perspective affords a specific place for the eremitic life as an extension of the cenobitic life and provides a specific assessment of the eremitic life in terms of its contribution to not only the monastic life, but to the Christian life, in general.[17] With regard to this contribution, in his work "St. Benedict and the Eremitical Life," Adrian Hastings argues that Benedict "fully accepted the traditional teaching on the relation of the cenobitical and eremitical lives as found in Cassian, and therefore, most likely, made provision at Monte Cassino for some of his elder monks to 'go out well-armed from the ranks of the community to the solitary combat of the desert.'"[18] Regardless of whether this was the case, the standing of the eremitical life is further enhanced in the first rule by St. Benedict's use of comparison. By contrasting the eremitic life to the two remaining forms of practice he addresses here, that of the

---

17. See Corcoran, "Wild Bird, with God in the Center," 148–49. Butler, *Benedictine Monachism*, 392, writes: "There is no historical justification for the thesis that St. Benedict intended his Rule, even in theory, to be a preparation for the eremitical life. He no doubt retained his admiration for that life as, in the abstract, the highest expression of the monastic life; but in the concrete he did not look on it as in practice even the theoretical ideal for his monks." See also de Vogüé, "Rule of Saint Benedict," 73, who writes, "Whatever his own ideas may have been concerning the relationship between the life of the cenobium and the eremitical life, which Cassian had analysed in more than one way, he certainly had a very great esteem for the contemplative spirituality of the hermit, and he urged his own cenobites not only to admire it platonically, or to make their asceticism a preparation for it; he also urged them to put into practice, here and now, some of its most characteristic realities." Colegate, *Pelican in the Wilderness*, 121, offers this brief observation about the provision provided in the first rule of the *Rule of St. Benedict*: "Subsequent Christian hermits, mistrusted as they sometimes were by their institutional superiors and vulnerable to outside skepticism or mockery, found in this provision their authentication."

18. Hastings, "St. Benedict and the Eremitical Life," 192.

sarabaites and of the gyrovagues, St. Benedict locates a stable place for the eremitic life. Neither form, that undertaken by the sarabaites nor that by the gyrovagues, has a longstanding role or place according to St. Benedict.[19]

Today, Camaldolese Benedictines interpret the first rule of the *Rule of St. Benedict* in a manner that honors and enables a plurality of forms of practice. The *Camaldolese Constitutions and Declarations to the Rule of Saint Benedict* is the legislation that guides their interpretation and application of the *Rule of St. Benedict*.[20] The most current version of the *Camaldolese Constitutions and Declarations* was formulated in response to the call to renewal issued in Vatican Council II, and select teachings regarding the eremitic practice will be considered in the discussion here.[21]

The scriptural foundation of the monastic life, as well as the place of both the cenobitic and eremitic forms, as affirmed in the *Rule of St. Benedict*, is emphasized in the *Camaldolese Constitutions and Declarations of the Rule of St. Benedict*.[22] In accordance with the foundational emphasis on the cenobitic and eremitic forms of practice established by St. Benedict, in the Camaldolese Benedictine tradition the monk may live the contemplative life in either the hermitage or the monastery.[23] Both forms receive descriptive and juridical treatment in the first two parts of the *Camaldolese Constitutions and Declarations*. Moreover, the relationship between both forms of practice is presented as one that is embedded in a distinctive feature of the Romualdian reform and of the Camaldolese Benedictine tradition, namely, the threefold good. The threefold good, also referred to as the threefold advantage, was articulated by St. Bruno-Boniface in the tenth century as the

---

19. For discussion of the relationship between this rule and St. Romuald's own practice, see Ward, "Relationship between Hermits and Communities," 54–63; see also Camaldolese hermit, *In Praise of Hiddenness*, 79–108. With regard to St. Benedict's attitude towards the gyrovagues in particular, see Wilkins, "On Hermits and Pilgrim Monks," 213–20.

20. See Matus, trans., *Constitutions and Declarations to the Rule of Saint Benedict*, 3: "The Camaldolese legislation consists of two distinct and interwoven parts: the constitutions proper, which are approved by the Holy See and may be changed only with its consent, and the declarations to the constitutions, which may be modified by the general chapter of the congregation."

21. On the call for renewal by Vatican Council II, see Barnhart, "Monastic Wisdom."

22. In clear terms the scriptural foundation of the monastic life is established by appeal to 1 Cor 12:4. For the purpose of brevity, henceforward the *Constitutions and Declarations of the Rule of St. Benedict* (2000) will be referred to as *Camaldolese Constitutions and Declarations*.

23. *Camaldolese Constitutions and Declarations* I.1.5.

distinct charism of the Order. It has been retained in the *Camaldolese Constitutions and Declarations*: "The Camaldolese tradition is characterized by the unity of the monastic family in the threefold good of *coenobium, solitudo*, and *evangelium paganorum* [community, solitude, evangelization]."[24] The threefold good creates a life marked by contemplation and action,[25] by possibilities for reclusion and opportunities for communion,[26] as it embodies elements of the coenobitical and eremitical foundation. The threefold good serves as a characteristic and defining statement of Camaldolese Benedictine life and practice.

In the Camaldolese Benedictine tradition, the common foundation of the hermitage and monastery serves as the shared basis of the common, primary goal of contemplation. In chapter 1, "The Spiritual Nature and Juridical Structure of the Camaldolese Congregation," of the *Camaldolese Constitutions and Declarations* it reads: "In both hermitage and monastery the monks attend to the contemplative life above all else."[27] The contemplative life is characterized in a way that heightens both what the monk does and the manner in which a given task, duty or practice is undertaken. Thus, while the monk undertakes a daily schedule that includes work, prayer, and worship, these practices become contemplative when they are infused by a certain quality of attentiveness and orientation. Such attentiveness, as a process whereby the monk listens, hears, and is guided by the divine, is suggested in these terms from the *Camaldolese Constitutions and Declarations*: "In his work, as in his practice of Christian mortification and ardent prayer, let him open his heart to the attentive hearing and meditating of God's word, which is the support of faith, the food of the soul, the pure and unfailing source of life in the Spirit (cf. DV 21–26)."[28] The contemplative life, described in these terms, orients the monk toward a progressively deepening awareness of, and union with, the divine presence.

Such progression in the contemplative life was articulated in St. Bruno-Boniface's interpretation of the threefold good. St. Bruno-Boniface understood the threefold good in terms that, themselves, suggest a progression of stages: "the life of the monastery, which is what novices want;

---

24. Ibid., I.1.3. See also Hale, "*Koinonia*: The Privilege of Love."
25. See Belisle, *Privilege of Love*, 10–13.
26. Ibid., 155.
27. *Camaldolese Constitutions and Declarations* I.1.4. See also Belisle, "'Hermit' Archetype," 41–50.
28. Ibid.

The Threefold Good

golden solitude, for those who are mature and thirst for the living God; and the preaching of the Gospel to the pagans, for those who long to be set free and to be with Christ."[29] St. Bruno-Boniface's insight is maintained in the *Camaldolese Constitutions and Declarations*; specifically, it appears in the willingness to be open to the possibility for the cultivation of monastic practice as consisting on a continuum, on a spectrum of developmental stages that acknowledges, and provides for, a plurality of forms of practice. The distinct forms of monastery and hermitage-tied to the needs of the novice and of the mature monk respectively-as defined specifically in section four of the first chapter of the *Camaldolese Constitutions and Declarations* indicate a relationship between the monastery and hermitage whereby life in the hermitage reflects an advanced stage of practice. This sentiment is expressly articulated in section 6 of chapter 1 of the *Camaldolese Constitutions and Declarations*. "In the monastery, the monk lives out his vocation day by day through union in charity with his brothers and through obedience to the Rule and the spirit of our tradition. Life in the monastery should be one of simplicity, solitude, and austerity so that the monks may not only progress in holiness but may be aided in their growth toward the life of the hermitage."[30] In the passage from the monastery to the hermitage, the monk undertakes movement from a primarily cenobitic practice towards a more strictly anchoritic one. Such movement is advised, not mandated. That is, it is an aspiration and not a requirement.

This move is defined in section 7 of chapter 1 of the *Camaldolese Constitutions and Declarations* where it reads that: "the Camaldolese hermitage is situated between the coenobitic and anchoritic ways of life. It keeps the best elements of both and creates a wise balance of solitude and life in common (cf. RVE ch. i)."[31] The location of the hermitage helps to orient both its specific role and its unique place in the Camaldolese Benedictine tradition. The section of this chapter continues: "Although the hermit remains united to his brothers and subject to the yoke of obedience (cf. RE no. 41; Op. XV, 18), he strives in solitary quiet to attain purity of heart and intimate union with God by means of greater mortification and more intense

---

29. See Wong, "Threefold Good," 81, who explains that the threefold good serves "as a concise expression of the Romualdian charism and Camaldolese identity."

30. *Camaldolese Constitutions and Declarations* I.1.6.

31. Ibid., I.1.7. See also *Camaldolese Constitutions and Declarations* I.2.11 on such a transfer as the fulfillment of monastic stability as aligned with the *Rule of St. Benedict* 1 and the *Rule of St. Benedict* 73.

and assiduous prayer."[32] Permission of the Prior is required for the monk to transfer from the monastery to the hermitage, and the transfer may be temporary or permanent.[33]

Camaldolese Benedictine hermitages are located in places where the contemplative life of solitude and silence may be cultivated.[34] The privacy of the community of hermits is safeguarded by canonical enclosure.[35] In his work *Love on the Mountain: The Chronicle Journal of a Camaldolese Monk*, Robert Hale, OSB Cam., author and Prior of the Hermitage at New Camadoli in Big Sur, California, explains that the eremitic spirituality of the community of hermits is embedded in the organization and placement of space. Fr. Hale writes that the Hermitage at New Camaldoli "consists of twenty-five small cottages, or cells, gathered around the three main community buildings, the chapel, library and refectory. And our schedule seeks to provide a balanced rhythm between moments of community and solitude, between prayer and work and rest. We gather four times a day for worship in community, at 5:45am for Vigils, 7am for Lauds, 11:30am for Eucharist and at 6pm for Vespers. We also gather for lunch, but breakfast and suppers may be taken either in common or in the solitude of the cell."[36] As a community of hermits, there are daily opportunities for communal as well as for solitary practice.

The Camaldolese Benedictine tradition emphasizes St. Benedict's insight that a more strictly anchoritic life may emerge from cultivation of the cenobitic life to the extent that this insight informs the structural foundation of Camaldolese Benedictine monastic practice. The Camaldolese Benedictines recognize that life in the hermitage may instill a desire for periods of more sequestered life and practice, and so they include the possibility for the hermit to cultivate eremitic life in reclusion, characterized as "an eminent form of monastic life and an excellent witness to the search for God in full freedom and communion, according to the saying of

---

32. *Camaldolese Constitutions and Declarations*, I.1.7.

33. For temporary transfers, see ibid., I.2.12; for permanent transfers, see ibid., I.2.15.

34. In *Camaldolese Constitutions and Declarations* I.4.96, it reads: "Our houses are to be established in appropriately secluded locations, so as to provide the community with the necessary climate of solitude and silence."

35. See *Camaldolese Constitutions and Declarations*, I.4.97.

36. Hale, *Love on the Mountain*, vii. Since this writing, the time for Vigils has been moved to 5:30am. Fr. Hale was Prior of the Hermitage from 1988–2000, and was re-elected in 2012; he also served as Prior (and was a co-founder) of Incarnation Monastery.

Camaldolese tradition."[37] As in the case of the monk who is called to cultivate eremitic practice in the hermitage, so too, in the case of the hermit who is called to reclusion, permission of the prior is required.[38] Reclusion entails a more isolated form of practice in which the monk withdraws further from the community. Though apart from the community, the recluse remains very much connected to the community "by unity of faith and charity."[39] Unity is further maintained through the recluse's obedience to the prior and to the community.[40] In this way, the recluse continues to serve and participate in and through the community. The *Camaldolese Constitutions and Declarations* maintain that "by enclosing himself within the narrow confines of a cell, the recluse imitates more closely the anchoritic life of the desert fathers. He represents a very high development of the monastic ideal, and in him the brothers find a model of life hidden with Christ in God."[41] As a result, the practice of the recluse is found to enhance, rather than detract from, the structural composition of the community as a community of hermits. Bound in unity and obedience, the recluse remains a member of this community who is distinguished by his form of practice.

Camaldolese Benedictine author Lino Vigilucci, OSB Cam., has suggested a depiction of the congregation with "the image of a wisely articulated pluralism which guarantees a variety of choices within the harmony of one monastic profession."[42] Pluralistic and harmonious, Fr. Vigilucci explains how this is both possible and desirable when he writes: "The Camaldolese institution with all its various components-cenobium and hermitage, reclusion and apostolate-has always enabled each person's character and balance

---

37. *Camaldolese Constitutions and Declarations*, I.4.105.

38. Ibid., I.1.7: "It is the prior who grants reclusion for brief or longer period of time. When a monk requests it, let the prior use discernment in giving his answer; above all let him remember that this particular experience of solitude demands a high degree of maturity and spiritual, psychological, and physical health. As for the monk, *amore libertatis inclusis*, his life of willing obedience is to be the primary manifestation of his freedom in Christ."

39. Ibid., I.4.105.

40. His obedience to the prior and to the community are also maintained through his relationship to the prior. See *Camaldolese Constitutions and Declarations*, I.4.105: "The prior shall show fatherly concern for the recluse by assisting him with frequent personal visits and guaranteeing him the necessary quiet. For his part, the recluse must know that he remains always united to the father of the community by obedience."

41. Ibid., I.1.7.

42. Vigilucci, *Camaldoli*, 141.

to develop harmoniously."[43] Openness to a range of possible expressions is, then, a means of providing both the individual and the community with the opportunity for living their vocation in the context of the Camaldolese Congregation.

Given the diversity of expression afforded the eremitic practice within the structure of the Camaldolese Benedictine Order in the *Camaldolese Constitutions and Declarations* that has been briefly outlined here, one might envision the relationship between the location of practice and the form of practice in this tradition in the following table:

Eremitic Practice in the Camaldolese Benedictine Tradition

Location of Practice	Monastery	Hermitage	Reclusion
Form of Practice	Cenobitic	Balances cenobitic and anchoritic	Strictly anchoritic practice

Depicted horizontally, one can see that life in either the monastery or in the hermitage is the primary, defining forms of practice in the Camaldolese Benedictine Order. Life in the monastery, as in Incarnation Monastery, located in the urban setting of Berkeley, California, is, as one can see from the connection through the vertical association, more closely cenobitic. In the monastery, the monks live and work together in a single house, coming together for daily prayer and mass. Life in the hermitage, as in New Camaldoli Hermitage, places more emphasis on withdrawal (*anachoresis*) from an urban setting. Here, the rural location, tucked about a mile in from a main highway on the California coastline, is intended to heighten opportunities for solitude and silence. Reclusion, although permitted as an expression of the anchoritic form, par excellence, is not a requirement of life in the hermitage but is, rather, a possible expression of such life.

The setting of the hermits at New Camaldoli Hermitage, while secluded, is not intended to be entirely isolationist. The hermits, like their monastic colleagues in an urban setting, cultivate considerable outreach. In accordance with the *Rule of St. Benedict*, their outreach assumes a variety of forms that may be adjusted according to local contexts and customs. Contemplative outreach through solidarity in prayer is an essential form. Most prominent within this form is solidarity with other members of the Church through the Eucharistic celebration. According to the *Camaldolese*

43. Ibid.

Constitutions and Declarations, "The sharing in God's life and the unity of His people are in fact given fitting expression and a mysterious realization in the Eucharist, in which the Church, made one with the sacrifice of Christ, offers herself to the Father."[44] In the Eucharist, as in their daily practices of individual and communal prayer, the monks and hermits are intimately connected with the Church.

For this reason, the contemplation of the hermits at New Camaldoli Hermitage is coupled with action.[45] Through works of charity, gospel witness, and hospitality, Camaldolese Benedictine monks and hermits participate in the apostolic work of the Church. Specifically, they bear witness "by living the monastic ideal and by sharing in the life and work of the community."[46] In this way, their witness has private and public, as well as individual and communal, dimensions within the community.

Just as the forms of solidarity are implemented by appeal to the *Rule of St. Benedict* and the founding fathers so, too, are these forms of monastic presence. Solidarity with the poor, through adherence to the evangelical vow of poverty, is found in the sharing of goods as the *Camaldolese Constitutions and Declarations* instruct that the monks "are to willingly set aside some part of their goods for the needs of the Church and for the sustenance of the poor; indeed, they are to love the poor with the tender affection of Christ, even to the extent of making sacrifices for them."[47] Through shared poverty, such solidarity extends and expands the outreach of the community of hermits to the larger community of the Church and beyond.

Hospitality, a central feature of the *Rule of St. Benedict*, is another prominent means of monastic presence. In this context, hospitality refers to both "material refreshment and accommodations to those who visit the community" as well as "spiritual nourishment in the fellowship of charity and in the encounter with God's word."[48] Both features emphasize what was, and remains, a distinctive application of Benedictine hospitality, namely, to welcome the guest as Christ himself.[49] For this reason, the sharing of material goods is undertaken in a spirit of communion; this same spirit infuses the sharing of spiritual guidance. In particular, retreat ministry is a prominent component of the contemplative and public outreach of the

44. *Camaldolese Constitutions and Declarations*, I.3.67.
45. Belisle, *Privilege of Love*, 23.
46. *Camaldolese Constitutions and Declarations*, I.6.122.
47. Ibid., 5.109.
48. Ibid., 6.124.
49. Fry, trans., *Rule of St. Benedict*, 53.

New Camaldoli Hermitage. Ecumenism is characterized as "an especially monastic way of responding to the Lord's call to preach the gospel"[50] in the *Constitutions and Declarations to the Rule of Saint Benedict*, and forms a distinctive ministry of the Camaldolese Benedictine community.[51] In this spirit, ecumenism extends to the cultivation of, and involvement in, inter-religious dialogue, as well as in the teaching and ministry found in a range of books and articles, and in conferences and speaking engagements.[52]

As we have seen, the organizational structure of the Camaldolese Benedictines allows for a diversity of practice within the life of the Camaldolese Order. This diversity is a characteristic feature of a rich and longstanding tradition, and it facilitates the attainment of one of the Order's stated aims that in the Camaldolese Benedictine way of life the monk's "outward form of life may be as consistent as possible with their inner reality."[53]

Eremitic Practice of the Camaldolese Hermits of Montecorona (Er. Cam.)

The *Constitutions of the Congregation of the Camaldolese Hermits of Montecorona* (2002) is the principal legislative document of the Camaldolese Hermits of Montecorona. The preface to these Constitutions orients the reader to the eremitic practice of these hermits and situates their practice in the context of the Camaldolese worldview. The *Rule of St. Benedict* "constitutes a fundamental code" for the hermits.[54] The reforms of St. Romuald, who renewed the eremitic life, are essential to their eremitic life.[55] As well, development according to the teaching of Blessed Paul Giustiniani distinguishes further, and in specific terms, the form of eremitic expression by the hermits.[56] The concluding section of the preface to the *Constitutions of Montecorona* highlights the intersection of the teachings and example of each of these three figures in the current practice of the hermits in an

---

50. *Camaldolese Constitutions and Declarations*, I.6.125.

51. Belisle, *Privilege of Love*, 24–26.

52. *Camaldolese Constitutions and Declarations*, I.6.125–26. See also Belisle, *Privilege of Love*, 24–26.

53. *Camaldolese Constitutions and Declarations*, 1.3.

54. See *Constitutions of the Congregation of the Camaldolese Hermits of Montecorona* (2002), preface 3.

55. Ibid.

56. Ibid., preface 6.

exhortation that reads: "May the solid food offered by Saint Benedict in his Rule, the luminous figure of Saint Romuald, the life and doctrine of our Founder, Blessed Paul Giustiniani, give us strength and light, a stimulus and encouragement on the path of the Gospel in the following of our Lord Jesus Christ, the supreme rule of our life and simultaneously its center and goal."[57] The *Constitutions of Montecorona* proper opens by situating the eremitic practice in the context of the Christian vocation of prayer. While all Christians are called to union with Christ through prayer, the hermit is called to make prayer the essential duty.[58] In order for this to be accomplished, the hermit is required to withdraw from all distractions. Limitations on speech and an austere lifestyle are grounded in obedience, poverty and simplicity. Withdrawal forms a particular relationship to the universal church. This relationship is explained in the *Constitutions of Montecorona* by appeal to the work of Peter Damian, who wrote St. Romuald's life and handed on his teachings. Among the many teachings Peter Damian includes is this one which regards the relationship between the hermit and the ecclesiastical community of which he is a member: "Material solitude does not impede but rather reinforces mysteriously the spiritual presence of the solitary in the community of believers. If the hermit prays, it is the Church that prays in him."[59] This explanation serves to define and to locate the place and, more specifically, the role of the solitary in the broader community of Christian believers. According to the *Constitutions of Montecorona*, all hermits are consecrated and bound by the evangelical counsels of poverty, chastity and obedience. Conversion of manners forms the foundation of the hermit's vows. Prayer and contemplation are defining features of the hermit's life.

The *Constitutions of the Congregation of the Camaldolese Hermits of Montecorona* are divided into three sections that address the hermit, the eremitical community, and the congregation, respectively. Here, the order of presentation further emphasizes the presence and role of the individual eremitic life within the broader contexts of the hermitage and the Church. The *Constitutions of the Congregation of the Camaldolese Hermits*

57. Ibid., preface 7.
58. Ibid., I.1.8.
59. Ibid., preface, 3. There is a significant relationship between the hermit and the Church, and perhaps it could be conceived in terms of a mutual reciprocity of support. While this section of the *Constitutions* emphasizes the role of the hermit as a member of the Church, this is certainly not to the exclusion of other expressions of this relationship. Ch. 4, "Wordless Preaching," of this work takes up the question of the hermit's role in the life of the Church through examination of the teachings of Don Paul Giustiniani.

Seeking in Solitude

of Montecorona qualify Romualdian eremiticism as a "harmonious fusion" of the cenobitic and anchoritic forms of practice.⁶⁰ As Dom Jean Leclercq explains in *Alone With God*, a study of Don Paul Giustiniani's teachings and writings about the eremitic life, "The fact that hermits live together gives them the opportunity to practice both fraternal charity and poverty. But their eremitic ideal imposes on them the duty of accepting the most rigorous implications of utter poverty which should be one of the characteristic features of their life."⁶¹ From the cenobitic practice, the hermits adhere to the *Rule of St. Benedict*, with its constructions of authority and of a common life.⁶² From the anchoritic practice, the hermit maintains solitude and silence by dwelling apart in a single cell.⁶³

The cell is the center of eremitic life for the hermit. It is characterized in vivid terms in the *Constitutions of the Congregation of the Camaldolese Hermits of Montecorona* as "the vital element of his spiritual progress."⁶⁴ The cell is the principal site for the hermit's prayer and contemplation. Prayer, cultivation of solitude and silence, *lectio divina*, and some forms of manual labor are among the activities undertaken by the hermit in the cell. Hermits also normally eat alone in their cells.⁶⁵ The *Constitutions of the Congregation of the Camaldolese Hermits of Montecorona* emphasize that it is "above all the lesson of humility which the solitude of the cell imparts" as the hermit "freed from blinding distractions . . . begins to see himself in the light of God and to take the measure of his own emptiness and his own imperfection."⁶⁶

As indicated in the *Constitutions of the Congregation of the Camaldolese Hermits of Montecorona*, the hermitage or cell is the principal site

---

60. Ibid., I.1.11.

61. Leclercq, *Alone with God*, 141.

62. *Constitutions of the Congregation of the Camaldolese Hermits of Montecorona*, I.1.11.

63. Ibid.

64. Ibid.

65. Ibid., I.3.36.

66. Ibid., I.3.33. See Camaldolese hermit, *In Praise of Hiddenness*, 11, who notes that the principle difference in comparison with Cistercian and Benedictine space in these terms: "This difference lies principally in the absence of a cloister and the juxtaposition of the solitary cells with their little garden. These, together with the church, the chapter room, the refectory, and the common utilities, constitute our universe, the place where we live, and give it typically, in effect, the aspect of a little village or, if you prefer, of a Palestinian laura. This setup goes back to St. Romuald himself."

for leading the eremitic life. As one hermit writes, "There is nothing more necessary for, and characteristic of, the hermit than to remain constantly in his hermitage. The hermitage is the determined space of the hermit's experience, which is marked by solitude, silence, prayer, and fasting."[67] The space of the hermitage, then, is marked by both its location and its function; it is a holy place of encounter.

Bound by adherence to shared constitutions and customs, as well as to the common vow of obedience, the life of the hermit also contains other elements of communal practice, however. The hermits share elements of a common schedule with, for example, a certain period of time each day given to manual labor and *lectio divina*. Regular occasions for confession of faults before the brethren, and absolution of such faults against the observance are other examples of practices pertaining to a common life. According to the *Customs of the Congregation of the Camaldolese Hermits of Montecorona*, in use by the hermits of Holy Family Hermitage, occasions on which there is a dispensation from silence are intended to "offer the possibility of a fraternal encounter to whoever desires it or may have need of it."[68] There is the possibility, as well, for those who choose, to participate in occasional, prescribed periods of recreation during which free conversation is permitted.[69]

According to the *Constitutions of the Congregation of the Camaldolese Hermits of Montecorona*, reclusion is a further form of the eremitic practice that may be cultivated for shorter or more extended periods, even perpetually, with permission. Reclusion "permits a stable union with God in an exceptionally intense manner"[70] and entails a life "of pure faith and of pure abandonment in God, more similar to Gethsemane than to Tabor."[71] Reclusion requires a hermit "of consummate virtue, of great humility and of notable human equilibrium."[72] The cell of the recluse, with a garden and surrounding wall, is further removed than the cells of the other hermits.[73]

---

67. Wencel, *Eremitic Life*, 113.

68. *Customs of the Congregation of the Camaldolese Hermits of Montecorona and the Ceremonial for the Divine Office* (2009), VIII.63.

69. Ibid., VIII.63–66. The dispensation from silence is an opportunity to communicate material or spiritual needs to the appropriate person(s) in VIII.64.

70. *Constitutions of the Congregation of the Camaldolese Hermits of Montecorona*, I.5.76.

71. Ibid.

72. Ibid., I.5.77.

73. Ibid., I.5.78. It is important to note that all cells have a walled garden.

Stability of place is more strictly undertaken. The recluse embraces "perpetual and inviolable silence" except for a weekly visit of the Prior and whatever contact with the others the Prior may deem necessary.[74] Here, too, the solitude of the recluse does not cut him off from the community, as he is still in relationship in several significant ways. Specifically, the practice of obedience and the vow of stability bind the recluse to the others in his community. The recluse, like his fellow hermits, remains subject to obedience in all of its forms, including obedience to the members of his community, and to those governing and guiding precepts. The Prior oversees the recluse; in this capacity, relationship in community is extended to the recluse and to the site of reclusion. Furthermore, the recluse follows the *horarium* of the other hermits; in this way, he is in solidarity and fellowship with the other members of his community as well as with the members of the universal Church as he celebrates Mass, says the liturgical hours, and conducts *lectio divina*.

Given these parameters for the eremitic practice in the *Constitutions of Montecorona* one might envision its depiction in the following table.

Eremitic Practice in the Camaldolese Hermits of Montecorona

Location of Practice	Entire Hermitage	Cell of Reclusion
Form of Practice	Semi-anchoritic with elements of cenobitism	Strictly anchoritic practice

Here, as in the organizational structure of the Camaldolese Benedictines considered earlier, there is a clear relationship between the space and form of the eremitic practice. Withdrawal from urban, populated areas is a requisite feature of the hermits of Montecorona. It is in such selective withdrawal that silence and solitude are most effectively cultivated. Eremitic space is defined by these practices. This is particularly evident in this description of the eremitic space of the hermits at Holy Family Hermitage in Bloomingdale, Ohio: "The nine solitary cells stand, in original fashion, in a semicircle about the church, the true center of the hermitage. The church's octagonal shape recalls the eighth day of Christ's resurrection and of eternity."[75] The hermits are removed from one another by life in their individual cells and

---

74. Unlike his fellow hermits, the recluse celebrates Mass and prays the divine office in his cell.

75. See Camaldolese Hermits of Monte Corona, Holy Family Hermitage, "Who Are the Camaldolese?" http://www.camaldolese.org/pages.php?pageid=1.

are brought together through adherence to a common rule and guidelines, as well as through union with the Church.

The relationship between the individual solitude of the hermit and solidarity with others is a defining feature of the eremitic practice of these hermits. The solitude of the Camaldolese Hermits of Montecorona is characterized by one hermit as "concealment in ecclesial communion."[76] This feature is evident in the form of witness that is attested to by others in, and beyond, the Church community. United by a shared understanding and cultivation of vows of stability and obedience, the Camaldolese hermit is always in communion with his fellow monks, and with the larger communities of the Church and the world. The Camaldolese hermit ministers to the world through his prayer and contemplation.[77] In an essential way, these contribute to the ways in which the hermit participates in the cross of Christ.[78]

Camaldolese Unity: Shared Principles

With regard to post-Vatican Council II reforms and developments of the Camaldolese Benedictine Order, Emanuele Bargellini, former Prior General, writes, "From the sixteenth century down to our own days, the development of the hermitage/monastery dialectic has underlined an emblematic point of this journey, as though it were the problem par excellence of Camaldolese history. The hermitage/monastery relationship stands at the heart of Camaldolese monastic experience. Inherited by St. Romuald, mostly through ancient eastern monasticism, it expresses a constitutive tension of monastic life focused around two polarities: community/individual

---

76. See Camaldolese hermit, *In Praise of Hiddenness*, 51.

77. Ibid., 65. Here the author describes the place of this vocation to the Church and to the world in these terms: "We have not been begotten by our holy father Romuald to take up a specific 'service' in the Church . . . But this does not mean at all that our solitary life is not, in a certain sense, a ministry, as is every other form of life that wants to be faithful to the Gospel. Prayer is our sacrifice, the contemplation of God our silent witness-yes, all this-and we must thus live intensely for the world of men, our brothers. And then Life will overflow into the Church and humanity."

78. Wencel, *Eremitic Life*, 16: "By choosing solitude a Christian takes the side of the mysterious and deep dimension of life which has been revealed in Christ's Cross. And what has been shown in the Cross is the mystery of love of the Trinity, the mystery of forgiveness and mercy. The Cross points to the direction and final aim of the Christian way of life. In any case, the Christian's final destination is a community of love." For another discussion of this, see Camaldolese hermit, *In Praise of Hiddenness*, 62–69.

and unity/pluralism."⁷⁹ A relationship of interconnectedness between the hermitage and the monastery is clearly embedded not only in the practices and lives of those in the New Camaldoli Congregation but also in those of the Camaldolese Hermits of Monte Corona. In both, the distinct structural expressions of the Camaldolese charism maintain a place for the eremitic form of life that is not at the expense of the community. Indeed, it is noteworthy that the particular emphasis of each expression continues to uphold the distinctiveness of the hermitage and the monastery in a way that provides flexibility and a place for the vocation of the individual without sacrificing community.⁸⁰ The particular relationship between cenobitic and eremitic elements in Camaldolese life and practice results in a unique, clearly constructed balance as communal prayer and worship accompany, and are accompanied by, silence and solitude. Camaldolese life and practice is neither entirely eremitic nor entirely cenobitic, as it is directly and simultaneously both.

---

79. Bargellini, "Concluding Remarks," 183.

80. This observation is expressed clearly with specific attention to the Congregation of New Camaldoli by Vigilucci, *Camaldoli*, 155, who writes that "with its particularity of cenobitical and eremitical life, or reclusion and apostolate, the Congregation of Camaldoli today shows itself in all its variety, fully respectful of the freedom with which the Spirit draws each person."

3

Remembering in Silence

The American Carthusians

He applied himself to righteousness as much as he could. He became an unassuming hermit.[1]

In the world he lived close to God. He rejected everything and became a poor hermit for the Lord.[2]

THE 2006 DOCUMENTARY FILM *INTO GREAT SILENCE* FEATURES LIFE IN THE Grande Chartreuse, the motherhouse of the Carthusian monastic order located in the French Alps.[3] In an early scene, the film highlights the face of a monk gazing into the camera, a look of calm and serenity in his eyes. The screen then turns black as the words from 1 Kings 19:11–13 appear in white print, affirming that the Lord came to Elijah not in sound or in spectacle, but in silence. The scene then shifts back to the same monk at prayer in his cell. It is early morning and heavy snowflakes fall on the monastery and surrounding mountains. A bell tolls and echoes the only sound breaking through the silence of the snowfall. As viewers of the film soon realized, silence and solitude would mark the remainder of this day, and the other days, filmed at the Carthusian monastery.[4]

1. This note and the next note refer to two of the contributions to the funeral parchment for St. Bruno, the founder of the Carthusian Order. For these and other contributions, see a Carthusian Monk, trans., *Saint Bruno as Seen by His Contemporaries*, 8. The parchment is taken from the Cathedral Chapter of Lyon, France.

2. Ibid., 20. The parchment is taken from Saint Peter's Monastery, Meaux, France.

3. *Into Great Silence*, DVD, Philip Gröning (Zeitgeist Films, 2006).

4. See Workman, *Evolution of the Monastic Ideal*, 252: "The history of the Carthusians

Seeking in Solitude

The opportunity for viewers to watch a film about life at the Grande Chartreuse is, quite simply, a remarkable one.[5] Public attention is exceptional for the Carthusians who pride themselves on their hiddenness. The Carthusians identify themselves as "heirs of the desert fathers" who live "the life of solitude and contemplation that once had been led by the monks of Egypt."[6] Like the Camaldolese and the Cistercians, the Carthusian Order was founded during a period of monastic reform in which many sought to reclaim a place and a role for the eremitic life and practice.[7]

The Carthusians who live in the Charterhouse of the Transfiguration in Arlington, Vermont reside in the only Carthusian Monastery for men in the United States. Although the monks have been living in the region since 1950, the Vermont Charterhouse was completed in 1970. It contains nine cells for brothers and eighteen cells for choir monks.[8] In accordance with Carthusian custom, the Vermont Charterhouse is located on a mountain in order to preserve the withdrawal and anonymity of the monks. Living in seclusion and devoting themselves to a life of prayer, the practice of the Vermont Carthusians on Mount Equinox is understood in the context of the church as a testimony to watchfulness and waiting as defined by the teachings in the statutes of their religious institute, the *Statutes of the Carthusian Order*.

---

is remarkable for its changelessness." See also Sciascia, *Silent Summer of 1944*, 2, where the author writes: "The founder of the Carthusians, St. Bruno, discovered the secret of contemplative life centuries ago: God is found in silence, God is silence, revealed in contemplation. In a recollected heart, it is he who speaks, revealing to cloistered souls the greatest mystery of love." The persistence of the silence of the monks in spite of torture and death is present in this account.

5. It is noteworthy that the film was received with excitement and curiosity by audiences across the United States. German documentary filmmaker Philip Gröning recognized that he was offered uncommon access to life in the Grande Chartreuse in order to make his film (see the description at the back cover of the DVD). Gröning was not alone in confronting a seemingly insurmountable challenge in his efforts to learn more about the Carthusians. See also Maguire, *Infinity of Little Hours*, also released in 2006, who found a similar challenge as she worked to gather information from former monks. The success of Gröning's film and Maguire's book indicate an interest in the lives of these monks that is hardly isolated. See Lockhart, *Halfway to Heaven*, xi: "The first edition of *Halfway to Heaven* was more popular than I could ever have imagined. Apart from being translated into a number of languages, it brought me hundreds of letters of appreciation from readers, many of these asking me to write more about the Carthusians." See also Pease, "Out of Great Silence."

6. Urban, "Carthusians Mark 900th Anniversary," 3.

7. For the Camaldolese Congregations, see ch. 2; for the Cistercian Order, see ch. 4.

8. See Schlegel and Hogg, *Monasticon Cartusiense*, 12.

This chapter examines some of the distinctive efforts of the Vermont Carthusians to define their hiddenness as described and discussed in sources authored by members and non-members of the Order. Like their fourth century predecessors, Carthusians define their monastic life and practice, in part, through their physical withdrawal from public life. Withdrawal means neither neglect of, nor isolation from, the world, however, as the Carthusians like their predecessors envision their practice, in part, in service to others. Through their monastic practice, these monks create a Carthusian desert; their practice requires intentional acts of remembering and living in accordance with the example set by the desert fathers so that their desert, the site of their hiddenness, is transformed space. In this chapter, we'll look more closely at two ways in which this Carthusian desert and as such, Carthusian hiddenness, is imagined. First, we will consider the mapping of physical space through the construction of the monastery; and second, we will look at the making of place through the activities of the hermitage cell.[9] As we will see, there are several ways the Carthusians draw on the example of their predecessors to define their hiddenness in the creation of monastic space and hermitage place. Through the adoption and adaptation of architectural models for the monastery and the cultivation of contemplation and prayer in the cell, the Vermont Carthusians structure hiddenness in terms established by their predecessors. Furthermore, like their fourth century counterparts, Carthusian hiddenness at the Charterhouse of the Transfiguration rests on, and is protected by, relationships of mutual support between monks, and between monks and society, founded on and maintained by voluntary, reciprocal, cooperative sharing of resources. Consideration of these features not only demonstrates how the Carthusian desert is being created and sustained on American soil but also contributes to an understanding of how this form of eremitic life and practice is being interpreted and defined in the contemporary, postmodern landscape of the United States.

The Carthusian Order

The Carthusian Order was founded during the spirit of monastic reform in the eleventh century. It is in this context that the origin of the Order is most

---

9. We might consider here a connection to the definition of place proposed by Inge, *Christian Theology of Place*, 68, who writes, "Places are the seat of relations and of meeting and activity between God and the world."

often situated in historical accounts. A brief statement of the history of the Carthusian Order is found in the work of Dom David Knowles, a historian of Christian monasticism. In his work, Knowles writes that the founding of the Carthusian Order originates in the life of St. Bruno of Cologne who first joined several hermits in the forest of Colan, and then left them to establish a group of hermits in 1084. Their hermitage site would later become part of the Grande Chartreuse, the motherhouse of the Carthusian Order.[10] Several letters from St. Bruno reflect his efforts to continue to encourage and support these hermits while he was founding another monastery in Calabria, Italy, outside of Rome.[11]

The customs of the Carthusians were codified under Guiges I, who served as Prior of the Order from 1110–36 CE, and a system of general chapter meetings and regular visitations was put in place.[12] In his assessment, Knowles writes that the Carthusians "resembled the Camaldolese, whom they may have consciously imitated, by living as hermits and meeting only at a few set times, but from the first their cells were built around a cloister to which the oratory was contiguous, and the whole complex was surrounded by a wall."[13] While the question of Carthusian imitation may be debated, it is the case that the Carthusians were among those who embraced the spirit of monastic renewal in the eleventh century and still survive today.

The eremitic impulse and orientation preserved by the Carthusians has several distinctive and differentiating elements. In his study of select monastic Orders, Tudor Edwards observes that there is a lack of compromise of the eremitic spirit that remains a hallmark of the Carthusian Order. Edwards suggests that, for the most part, of the Orders that emerged in the eleventh century that sought a recovery of the eremitical impulse "the original tendency to be purely eremitical was soon coloured by a

---

10. Knowles, *Christian Monasticism*, 65.

11. See, e.g., Saint Bruno, *Two Letters and the Profession of Faith*. Encouragement and exhortation are particularly evident in the second letter in this publication, "A Letter of St. Bruno to the monks of the Grande Chartreuse, France, written from the Hermitage of the Tower in Calabria, Italy at about 1099," 7–9. For discussion of tensions caused by the emergence of Carthusian life and practice in the context of medieval monasticism, see Conley, "Eremitical Anthropology of William of St. Thierry," 116, who writes: "Inspired by the primitive Egyptian solitude of the early monks, the Carthusians resurrected the eremitical ideal as a powerful alternative to the more communitarian models of monastic life in the medieval period."

12. Knowles, *Christian Monasticism*, 122.

13. Ibid., 66.

compromise combining Benedict's Rule with the precepts of the Desert Fathers. The Carthusians, however, remained solitaries, or as near to being solitaries as any monks ever came. Each reform initiated its own bye-laws or what might be regarded as a supplement to the original Rule."[14] Edwards' observation regarding the approach to reform in the Carthusian Order is just as evident today, as demonstrated by the structure and content of the current *Statutes of the Carthusian Order*.

A statement of the founding and development of the Carthusian Order opens the prologue to the *Statutes of the Carthusian Order* and provides information about the principles that guide the practice of Carthusian monks. After Guiges I, under Prior Anthelm, the first General Chapter was assembled at the Grande Chartreuse "to which all the Houses-the Grande Chartreuse included-pledged themselves in perpetuity."[15] The General Chapter served an essential role in the stability and structure of the Order. By the time of the Council of Trent, the Order operated with three collections of ordinances, reduced to the New Collection of the Statutes. Several editions were approved over the years prior to the Second Vatican Council. In accordance with the council's call for a renewal of the contemplative way of life, "the General Chapter of 1971 approved and promulgated the Renewed Statutes, which were revised and corrected with the co-operation of all the members of the Order."[16] These were revised again twelve years later with the *Revised Code of Canon Law* (1983) and were approved at the General Chapter (1989). The *Statutes of the Carthusian Order* were divided into two groups: Books 1–4 are the *Constitutions of the Carthusian Order*, and Books 5–9 are the earlier *Statutes* included for the purpose of institutional memory. Such division marks more than a mere acknowledgement of the accretion of teaching over time; rather, it recognizes the role that such teaching has in forming and shaping a community of hermits and does so in a way that intentionally honors the past as a site for continuing interpretation and application in the present as well as in the future. As the *Statutes of the Carthusian Order* most eloquently state with regard to the sustained inclusion of the earlier teachings: "We do not, however, wish the earlier Statutes, especially the more ancient, to be forgotten; rather we desire that, although they no longer have force of law, their spirit may

---

14. Edwards, *Worlds Apart*, 21.

15. *Statutes of the Carthusian Order* 1.1.1. See also Merton, trans., *Solitary Life*. On Prior Anthelm, who died in 1178, see Carthusian monk, *Carthusian Saints*, 7–9.

16. Ibid.

live on in our present observance."[17] Perhaps this statement serves also to frame the orientation of the Carthusian monks not only to questions of self-identity in the present, but also to concerns about reform and renewal in the future.

In her recent work on the Carthusian charterhouse, Carol Steyn writes that "there are today nineteen charterhouses for monks, with a total of 370 monks."[18] Each Carthusian monastery houses approximately twenty monks. Two types of Carthusian monks live in the charterhouse, the choir monks (or priests, called fathers) and the brothers. The distinction applies, in part, to a division of labor with regard to the material needs of the monastery and of the monks.[19] Each type of monk gives a specific form of service. Choir monks spend most of the day in the hermitage except for Mass and prayer and a weekly walk. As described by Cori Fugere Urban in the article "Carthusians Mark 900th Anniversary of Founder's Dies Natalis," which appeared in the *Vermont Catholic Tribune*, the Carthusian brothers "also live a life of solitary prayer and share in the communal prayers and Mass in the chapel. They are responsible for taking care of the material needs of the monastery, so their life complements the life of the fathers who are not permitted to leave their cells to work. It is the dedicated life of the brothers that makes the fathers' life in cell possible."[20] This distinction, based as it is in part in a division of labor, also suggests that there may be a qualitative difference between the types of isolation lived by each category of monks.

Withdrawal to the Mountain

The Vermont Carthusians define their hiddenness, in part, through their physical withdrawal from public life. As is the Carthusian custom, such withdrawal is defined by the remote, largely less accessible location of the charterhouse. The history of the Vermont Carthusians suggests that efforts to secure such a location for their charterhouse took time, and that concern with withdrawal was a factor in securing a foundation. The mapping of a Carthusian space, also referred to as a Carthusian desert, is a collaborative undertaking. From topographical considerations about charterhouse

---

17. Ibid.

18. Steyn, "Charterhouse of Nonenque," 10.

19. See Urban, "Carthusians Mark 900th Anniversary," 5. See also Steyn, "Charterhouse of Nonenque," 2.

20. Ibid., 5.

Remembering in Silence

location to the minute details of the monastic cell, the construction of a Carthusian desert in which the Carthusian vocation may be realized, requires sustained material and immaterial support.[21]

This is illustrated well in the story of the founding, construction, and maintenance of the Charterhouse of the Transfiguration, the home of the Vermont Carthusians. The story of their founding begins in the mid-twentieth century, a period of deep social, cultural, and religious change in the United States. It is a tale of collaboration, shared resources, and trust. It has been told by several persons including Robert Hoguet, a Catholic layperson who, with his wife Louise, was closely involved in the establishment.[22] Robert Hoguet records the story of the early stages of the founding of the Carthusian charterhouse in his autobiography. In 1950, the Carthusian Father Thomas Verner Moore (Dom Pablo Maria) communicated his intention to found a Carthusian monastery in the United States to his friends, Robert and Louise Hoguet.[23] The Hoguets, who were in a position to provide financial resources and to appeal to select, key members of the Catholic hierarchy, spent several months investigating the possibility. Describing their efforts in his memoir, Robert Hoquet writes: "At that time, although the idea was favorably considered, we were assured by all concerned that nothing could be determined upon until after the next general chapter of the Carthusian Order, to be held in April 1951. But shortly after the invasion of Korea, and perhaps as a consequence thereof, a change of heart took place, and we were advised that an immediate foundation was being considered. My wife, in fact, was asked to look for a site, which she did, visiting various estates on Long Island and elsewhere."[24] Funds also needed to be secured.

A farm of several hundreds of acres in Whitingham, Vermont was donated by Elizabeth Pierce in spring 1951.[25] Such a donation would prove

---

21. Carthusian monk, *Poor therefore Rich*, 147, and ch. 79 of the *Customs* addresses this. Like their fourth-century counterparts, the twenty-first-century Carthusians are intimately dependent on others within and outside the enclosure of the monastery.

22. I am grateful to have learned, late in the composition of this book, about the publications of two authors who have written brief historical accounts of the founding of the Charterhouse of the Transfiguration and on the Carthusian Order in the United States. For more details about the founding of the Charterhouse, please see the essays in Emery and *Analecta Cartusiana, Charterhouse of the Transfiguration: Two Historical Essays.*

23. For a succinct account of the founding of the Carthusian charterhouse in the United States that discusses the role of Fr. Thomas Verner Moore, see Neenan, *Thomas Verner Moore*, 228–35.

24. Hoguet, *Robert Louis Hoguet*, 168.

25. Ibid., 169. On p. 173, the author describes a visit to the site in August of 1952 during which he saw that the construction of the hermitages was in progress.

essential to the founding of the Vermont Charter, and was in keeping with the teachings of the *Carthusian Statutes*. Sky Farm was approved on April 24, 1951 by the general chapter as the site for the Order.[26] A small group of priests and brothers lived there for ten years during which "the community grew slowly, acquiring more property and building a few primitive huts to be used as hermitages until the permanent monastery could be built."[27] The acreage also grew during this period through subsequent donations.[28]

While ideal in some respects, the monks determined that a state highway brought too much traffic too close to the Whitingham site and challenged their purpose to remain "far removed from contact with the exterior world."[29] Another donation of land allowed them to better attain their desired hiddenness. The foundation was moved to Mount Equinox in 1960.[30] Using an existing building on the grounds that "contained central rooms, kitchen facilities, and many suites" the building served as a "suitable structure for a temporary Carthusian charterhouse. Cubicles designed for transient skiers became hermitages for the monks."[31] During this time,

---

26. "Carthusians in America," n.p. See also Urban, "Carthusians Mark 900th Anniversary."

27. "Carthusians in America," n.p. See also Lockhart, *Halfway to Heaven*, 106: "In the early days of the American Carthusian community, while the Brothers lived in the farmhouse the Fathers lived in little shanties they had built in the woods round about, reminiscent of Bruno's original band of Carthusians. The monastery was set up in one of the coldest parts of America."

28. Ibid.

29. "Early Times: The Sixties," n.p. The purpose of the change of location pertained to seclusion. One of the principle features of Carthusian desert (as defined by Carthusians) is hiddenness. The desire for hiddenness rests at the heart of the founding of the Carthusian monastery on Mt. Equinox.

30. Urban, "Carthusians Mark 900th Anniversary." See also Lockhart, *Halfway to Heaven*, 107, who describes the intention of the donation in these terms: "The owner, a childless millionaire from one of America's leading chemical combines, was fearful that the beautiful forest land he had acquired on his retirement would be spoilt by commercial developers after his death. He felt that in the hands of the Carthusians, whose way of life had not changed through the centuries, his beloved nature reserve which abounded in wildlife would remain equally unchanged through the centuries to come." The donor was Dr. Joseph G. Davidson of the Union Carbide Corporation. The significance of the mountain as a religious archetype should be noted; this is a typical characteristic feature of Carthusian space.

31. "Early Times: The Sixties," n.p., which reads: "One of Davidson's few mistakes-the construction of a building he once intended to use as a ski lodge-was put to good advantage. It contained central rooms, kitchen facilities, and many suites under its twelve gables, and thus became a suitable structure for a temporary Carthusian charterhouse.

plans for the construction of the monastery were underway. Victor Christ-Janer and Associates of New Canaan, Connecticut were responsible for the design of the monastery. Architects appealed to local architectural styles, another distinctive feature and practice of Carthusian construction, as Carol Steyn observes in her work on Carthusian architecture. Steyn writes that "the Carthusians, in their architecture, always adapted to the customs of the country, provided that the principle of extreme simplicity was not relinquished."[32] This practice informs the distinctiveness of style between charterhouses and reflects historical precedent.

In form, then, the Charterhouse of the Transfiguration is like other Carthusian monasteries. As Robert H. Mutrux observes in his work *Great New England Churches*, considerable attention was given to understanding Carthusian life and practice in the construction of the monastery. Mutrux writes that, with regard to the Carthusians, "their self-imposed way of life presented a difficult problem for the architect. Their habitation must be directed inward, not outward. It must serve the chapter and its members only and not invite intercourse with the general public. It was essential, above all else, to avoid the architectural expression of grandeur and human pride that, with rare exceptions, has been the mark of religious architecture throughout the ages."[33] The use of concrete and unpolished Barre granite had the effect of creating the desired space. Father Lorenzo Maria De La Rosa Jr., Prior of the Charterhouse of the Transfiguration, contends that such materials and craftsmanship "describes the characteristic elements of Carthusian life: permanence, austerity and rugged simplicity."[34] Such consideration and assessment assumes a real connection between the form and the function of the monastery. Underlying the architecture of the charterhouse is the belief that its external form betrays an internal aim, a belief that is embedded in the *Carthusian Statutes*[35] and is apparent in charterhouses around the world.

Cubicles designed for transient skiers became hermitages for the monks . . . Davidson began transferring land in fifty-acre parcels, for tax purposes, to the Carthusian Order. The eventual gift would total seven thousand acres."

    32. Steyn, "Charterhouse of Nonenque," 13, who cites Dimier, *Les Moines Batisseurs*, 101.
    33. Mutrux, *Great New England Churches*, 101.
    34. Urban, "Carthusians Mark 900th Anniversary," 5.
    35. *Statutes of the Carthusian Order* 1.1.1.

Enclosure of the Charterhouse and Anonymity of the Hermitage Cell

The architecture of the Charterhouse of the Transfiguration, like Carthusian charterhouses around the world, is intended to create a place wherein, according to author Robert Mutrux, the monks are able "to reside in an atmosphere of complete isolation."[36] Like many of their fourth century predecessors, Carthusians strive to cultivate solitude and contemplation continuously. Carthusians espouse "strict dedication to a hidden life of prayer and contemplation in the silence and solitude of the hermitage, radical separation from the world, simplicity, poverty of spirit, penance, monastic vows especially conversion of life and obedience."[37] To this end, the Carthusian charterhouse is the site of a community wherein each individual monk lives guided by these principles.[38]

The Carthusian charterhouse is structured to accommodate both types of monks, the choir monks and the brothers, and to assure proper space for their respective forms of practice. It was decided early in the formation of the Carthusian Order that these needs were most appropriately met by adopting and adapting the early desert monastic *laura*, which was prominent in the Judean desert, as the architectural prototype for the charterhouse. "By definition, a *laura* is a monastery of recluses, each monk living alone in his cell, meeting with the others only on Saturdays and Sundays for prayer and to stock up on food and other necessities. The Greek term 'laura' means 'lane' and is apparently related to the location of the cells along a path leading to the main building. Every laura is composed of these two elements: the central building containing a church and other utilitarian structures, and the monks' cells."[39] The laura, employed in other eremitic

---

36. Mutrux, *Great New England Churches*, 101. See also Dimier, *Stones Laid before the Lord*, 186: "This way of life required a unique arrangement of the buildings, a radical departure from the monastic tradition."

37. Urban, "Carthusians Mark 900th Anniversary," 6.

38. See Dimier, *Stones Laid before the Lord*, 185: "Everything in a charterhouse is arranged so that the religious can spend the greater part of the day in solitude, recollection, and silence in their cells. The cenobite, particularly the Cistercian, lives from morning until night in the company of his brothers, whether in the common dormitory, the cloister, the library, the church for the Divine Office, the refectory, or the area for manual work. The Carthusian, in contrast, usually lives in his three-room cell, separated from everyone else."

39. Tsafrir, *Ancient Churches Revealed*, 153. See Edwards, *Worlds Apart*, 22, who observes that the distinctive architectural feature of the charterhouse is "the range of cells

Remembering in Silence

forms of practice including the Hermits of Bethlehem whom we will consider in chapter 5, allows for the necessary preservation of collective silence and individual solitude. Moreover, it enables a life of mutual support and encouragement in this shared endeavor; by dwelling in space that has been commonly mapped for these purposes, the monks are able to cultivate lives of simplicity and deep awareness, lives of prayer and contemplation.

According to the *Statutes of the Carthusian Order*, the place of the cell is the site of a deepening interiority of hiddenness. The interiority of hiddenness has a clear and central purpose. It is no surprise, then, that considerable attention is given to the cell in the first book of the rule of the order, the *Statutes of the Carthusian Order*. We might consider the teaching contained in chapter 4 of the first book of the *Statutes* which reads: "our principal endeavor and goal is to devote ourselves to the silence and solitude of cell. This is holy ground, a place where, as a man with his friend, the Lord and his servant often speak together; there is the faithful soul frequently united with the Word of God; there is the bride made one with her spouse; there is earth joined to heaven, the divine to the human. The journey, however, is long, and the way dry and barren, that must be traveled to attain the fount of water, the land of promise."[40] Here, explicit attention is directed to the hermitage cell as a sacred space, that is, in this context, as space that is constructed and defined by its purpose as a site of encounter and experience for the monk.[41]

The Carthusian hermitage is a simple two-storied structure.[42] Upon entering the hermitage through the one and only point of entry, there is a long hall called an ambulatory which divides the first floor into two uneven halves. The narrower half contains a series of rooms aligned in a single row. Each room has a designated purpose; the rooms are connected, although each room is accessible only from the ambulatory. Rooms are allotted for

---

or individual three-roomed houses opening out from three sides of the great cloister, with another cloister for the laybrothers' quarters . . . The Carthusian monastery thus resembled the *laura* of the desert hermits, and its plan is little altered even today."

40. *Statutes of the Carthusian Order* 1.4.1.

41. See Jasper, *Sacred Desert*, 36.

42. For a floor plan of a Carthusian hermitage, see Mutrux, *Architecture of Contemplation*, 8. See also the plans and images in Emery and *Analecta Cartusiana, Charterhouse of the Transfiguration: Two Historical Essays*. It is worth noting, as well, that the cell is often identified as a religious archetype for the tomb and/or the cave. For a brief statement of the development of the charterhouse with regard to its connection to local practice and custom, see also Knowles, *Christian Monasticism*, 198.

the placement of food, for chopping and storing wood that will be used to heat the hermitage, and for the work to be undertaken by the monk. The larger half contains the outdoor garden, also accessible only from the ambulatory. The garden is the length of the entire row of rooms across the ambulatory. A single stairway located in the middle of the first floor, leads from the first floor to the second floor. The second floor contains two rooms: the anteroom which contains an altar and space for prayer, and the main room or cubiculum which contains the stove, bed, table, chair, and toilet. Windows are found on both floors.

Perhaps such interior hiddenness transforms the monk so that his life is one of anonymity before God. Anonymity is an element of Carthusian identity that betrays itself in a variety of forms. One of the more obvious forms is the lack of self-identification in authorship; works authored by Carthusian monks are identified not by the birth or baptismal name of the individual monk but, rather, by the ascription, "A Carthusian." Such anonymity has the effect of emphasizing and elevating the form of life professed by the author as the identifying marker of authorship. Moreover, this practice with regard to authorship represents a contrast to the typical means of marking identity, ownership and accountability for one's work. Another, perhaps less obvious, form of anonymity is embodied in the practice and cultivation of silence. As one Carthusian observes, "Our silence is not just emptiness and death. On the contrary, it should draw ever nearer, and bring us nearer, to the fullness of life. We are silent because the words by which our souls would fain live cannot be expressed in earthly language."[43] Here, too, the practice of silence is a means of embracing a form of hiddenness. Likewise, there is an explicit purpose and end to the monk's cultivation of silence. According to one Carthusian contemplative silence is a means of listening. He writes that "silence calls for 'a tranquil listening of the heart that allows God to enter through all its doors and passages' (cf. 1.4.2). Silence is a listening: not the feverish expectation of a word that would strike our ears and fill our heart, but a calm receptivity to him who is present and who works noiselessly in our inmost being."[44] For this reason, as he later explains, "Silence is the work of God; but, it is much more than that, as we said: it is God's word."[45]

---

43. Carthusian monk, *They Speak by Silences*, 1.
44. Carthusian monk, *Wound of Love*, 63.
45. Ibid., 67.

Dwelling in Silence and Solitude

It is, perhaps, in the activities of the hermitage cell that the vocation of the Carthusian monk is most clearly and widely interpreted by others. Like their desert predecessors, Carthusians are believed to have a specific place, role and function in the global and local church communities through their lives of contemplation and prayer. As Father Lorenzo Maria De La Rosa Jr., Prior of the Charterhouse of the Transfiguration explains, "If we hope to be of benefit to the Church and world, we cannot see it other than living in fidelity and without compromise the charism bequeathed to us by St. Bruno and sanctioned by the mother Church."[46] Given the context of St. Bruno's life and the call to the eremitic practice that he followed, Fr. De La Rosa's statement of this interpretation of the distinctively Carthusian charism, of the Carthusian life of contemplation, may be understood as a form of presence before God. Another related perspective of the nature of this charism has been defined by one former postulant to the Carthusian Order in these terms: "It is a special characteristic of a Carthusian vocation that the soul should seek God and nothing else but God. God calls all men to seek Him above all creatures; but all men are not called in this life to seek God and God *alone* and to occupy themselves with *nothing else but God*."[47] Carthusian contemplation, as a means of being present to the divine in silence and in solitude, is the sole occupation of the Carthusian monk.

Fr. De La Rosa's remarks emphasize further how the Carthusian presence is interpreted by those in the context of the Roman Catholic Church. In practical terms, members of the Carthusian Order conduct lives of contemplative prayer, prayer that is possible precisely because of their withdrawal, isolation, and anonymity. In ecclesiastical terms, the vocation of the Carthusians is a specific form of imitation and witness. We may look briefly at how this has been defined by appeal to several key papal pronouncements and documents in chronological sequence issued during the papacy of Pope John Paul II (1978–2005).

---

46. Urban, "Carthusians Mark 900th Anniversary," 3. See also monk [anon.], *Hermitage Within*, 135: "This, then, will be your interior life in the hermitage: as continuously as you can, you will associate your personal acts with the three divine persons' song of glory and love, so that your own acts, assumed by Jesus Christ, may rise, infinitely precious, to God."

47. Carthusian retreatant, *Carthusian Life and Its Inner Spirit*, 10 (emphasis not mine); see also Ravier, *Saint Bruno the Carthusian*.

Seeking in Solitude

In an address that appeared on October 5, 1984, in commemoration of the 900th anniversary of the founding of the Carthusian Order, Pope John Paul II speaks directly to the monks about the role of their Order in the life of the Roman Catholic Church. The Pope calls on the monks to follow the example of their founder, St. Bruno, and to know that their role has an explicit location in the life of the Church. The Pope explains to the monks that "this specific and heroic vocation of yours does not put you on the margin of the Church. Rather it places you in its very heart. Your presence is a constant call to prayer, which is the premise of every authentic apostolate . . . The Church holds you in esteem, counts a great deal on your witness, and relies on your prayers...The world is watching you and, perhaps, unknowingly, expects a great deal from your contemplative life."[48] We might consider the themes of centrality and witness as they are present in Pope John Paul II's later pronouncements.

In his exhortation, *Vita Consecrata* (Consecrated Life), issued in 1996, Pope John Paul II clarifies the role served by those in the Roman Catholic Church who live the consecrated life including those vowed to a religious institute, such as the members of the Carthusian Order, whose lives are entirely devoted to the purpose of contemplation.[49] Here, the Pope affirms that those living the contemplative life offer a particular means of imitating Jesus Christ, who withdrew from others for the purpose of silence and solitude and who prayed on the mountain and in the desert in the presence of God the Father. In this way, according to the exhortation, the contemplative life bears witness to the example of Jesus Christ and attests to the pervasive love for God that is to be embodied in the Church. The Pope also emphasizes the connection between those who cultivate the contemplative life and other members of the Church through appeal to the idea of testimony. With regard to the testimony of the contemplative life, the Pope asserts that, "In solitude and silence, by listening to the word of God, participating in divine worship, personal asceticism, prayer, mortification and the communion of fraternal love, they direct the whole of their lives and all their activities to the contemplation of God. In this way they offer the ecclesial community a singular testimony of the Church's love for her Lord, and they contribute, with hidden apostolic fruitfulness, to the growth

---

48. Pope John Paul II, "God Alone Is the Source of True Peace," 9.

49. Pope John Paul II, *Vita Consecrata*. It is identified "as a further aid in our reflection" by the members of the Charterhouse of the Transfiguration, *Saint Bruno Pilgrim of the Absolute*, 6.

of the People of God."⁵⁰ As a testimony of love for God, through their single focus and undivided lives of prayer, those who live the contemplative life thus bear witness in a highly particular way.

Pope John Paul II had further occasion to emphasize this particularity with regard to the Carthusian role of bearing witness through their lives of contemplation in his address to the members of the Carthusian Order on the 900th anniversary of the death of their founder, St. Bruno, in 2001.⁵¹ Here, Pope John Paul II refers to the witness borne by the members of the Carthusian Order in these terms: "Untiring sentinel of the coming kingdom, seeking to 'be' before 'doing,' the Carthusian Order gives the Church strength and courage in her mission . . ."⁵² This mission is a transformative one, as it is directed beyond the materialism and individualism pervasive in many cultures and worldviews. The Pope drew further attention to the counter-cultural orientation of the Carthusians in his assertion that, "Your poverty offered for the glory of God and the salvation of the world is an eloquent protest against the logic of profit and efficiency that often close the hearts of men and nations to the real needs of their brothers. Your life hidden with Christ, like the silent Cross planted in the hearts of redeemed humanity, remains, for the Church and for the world, the eloquent sign and permanent reminder that every human being, today as yesterday, can let himself be captivated by Him who is only love."⁵³ The Carthusian witness to poverty and hiddenness is here upheld as both exemplary and necessary.

50. Pope John Paul II, *Vita Consecrata* 8. See also Knowles, *Christian Monasticism*, 199, where he writes that "pledged to a life of penance, solitude and prayer wholly apart from the world, without any concession to temporal interests and values, they are a standing witness to the unseen, and their vocation demands a very rare combination of spiritual, psychological and physical qualities."

51. This was the celebration of the Dies Natalis of St. Bruno. The Dies Natalis refers to the birth of new life of the individual in heaven.

52. See Pope John Paul II, *Captivated by Him Who Is Only Love*, 6.

53. Ibid., 7. The sentiment expressed by Pope John Paul II in these words appears to echo that of his predecessor, Pope Pius XI, who, in addressing the members of the Carthusian Order following revision of the Carthusian Statutes so as to be in conformity with the Code of Canon Law (1917) wrote: "For, if ever it was needful that there should be anchorites of that sort in the Church of God it is most specially expedient nowadays when we see so many Christians living without a thought for the things of the next world and utterly regardless of their eternal salvation, giving rein to their desire for earthly riches and the pleasures of the flesh and adopting and exhibiting publicly as well as in their private life pagan manners altogether opposed to the Gospel." This appears in Pope Pius XI, *Contemplatives in the Heart of the Church*, 9. This volume contains the English translation and Latin text of Pope Pius XI's Apostolic constitution *Umbratilem*, which was published on July 8, 1924.

Seeking in Solitude

The Carthusian interpretation of their testimony as a form of witness that contributes to the transformation of the world through the love of God is best understood by appeal to their own descriptions and explanations, that is, to their own expressions of that witness. As one Carthusian writes: "Our role in the Church is to be *a communion of solitaries for God*. To be men for God: that indeed is the first call that the Lord has made to us. And to be solitaries for God: all the details of our life show this to be our way. But we are not isolated solitaries; we are in the desert in communion with brothers who share the same ideal as ourselves. The task which each brother is trying to accomplish, hidden in his cell or in the silence of his workshop, is one that he shares with all his brothers: that of being consecrated to God in solitude. It is this task, at once single and shared, which unites us (cf. 3.4)."[54] These words express the Carthusian identity as one that is simultaneously both solitary in form and in solidarity with others.

For the Vermont Carthusians, this particular form of witness is manifest further and in a very specific manner in the context of their local church. As Father Mary Paul Chapeau, Vicar of the Charterhouse of the Transfiguration explains, "We are part of the Church of Vermont. Our role, our duty, is to pray for the people and to be present to God, to be representatives praying for the people."[55] Father Chapeau continues by stating that because many people are "very busy and don't mind about God, the Carthusians pray for their needs in a special way."[56] When asked about the specific value of their service to the world today, another member of the Carthusian community suggests, "There is a certain quality about Carthusian reclusion which is even greater than that of ordinary solitude and which seems to be lost when you open the door. Our silence can profit the world without speaking. There is a certain grace about the Carthusian vocation and it seems to me that fidelity to that grace brings more to the world and more to those seeking retreats than a slight watering down of our ideal for the sake of helping retreatants directly."[57] Here, the silence of the

54. Carthusian monk, *Wound of Love*, 49.

55. Urban, "Carthusians Mark 900th Anniversary," 6.

56. Ibid.

57. Lockhart, *Halfway to Heaven*, 109. Lockhart introduces the Prior as author of these words. See also Carthusian retreatant, *Carthusian Life and Its Inner Spirit*, 2: "Historically and de facto, Carthusian life is an attempt to bring into existence once again the life of the Fathers of the Desert, and to solve the problems of one who seeks a cave where he can be all alone with God, but can see no means of providing for himself in such a cave the necessary means of existence."

Carthusians is identified as a necessary contribution to the Roman Catholic Church and to the world.

The vocation of the Carthusians of the Charterhouse of the Transfiguration is presented as a form of spiritual patronage for the members of the global and local church. Patronage is never fully disinterested as it depends on mutual support: in this case, just as the monks-though hidden and anonymous-must have some awareness of the world from which they withdraw, so too those in the world seek some awareness of the monks. As one reporter writes of the Vermont Carthusians: "But they are conscious that their witness, and their role in the universal Church, goes beyond their responses to particular appeals for intercessory prayer. As one monk put it, contemplative prayer cannot be 'tied down' to any particular cause. The prayer and witness of these monks is as seamless and unchanging as the granite that surrounds them."[58] On occasion, and most especially with the founding and construction of the Charterhouse of the Transfiguration, these Carthusians receive material support from those who dwell outside the enclosure of their monastery for the maintenance of their vocation. In the case of the Charterhouse of the Transfiguration, the Carthusian desert is a socially constructed space that required the participation of many persons and resources. Its maintenance depends, to some extent, on the retention of this support.

A Carthusian Presence

Such observations on the part of Pope John Paul II, several Carthusians, and others, about the place and role of the Carthusian Order may begin to address what it might mean for the American Catholic Church that these monks manifest their hiddenness in the United States. Living in seclusion and devoting themselves entirely to prayer, the practice of the Vermont hermits is understood as a testimony to the cultivation of watchfulness and waiting. Thus, despite its unique adaptation to its specific location, in form, the Charterhouse of the Transfiguration is like other Carthusian monasteries in order that the monks can serve this purpose. As we have seen, the detachment and isolation of the Vermont Carthusians contributes in a recognized, and in a recognizable, way to the growth and development of the global and local church communities.

---

58. Lawler, "Silence and Solitude," 19.

And yet the issue of public disclosure with which this chapter opened is a pressing one. As one pilgrim, writing in 1958 observes, "The Carthusian of today holds the position of a *ne plus ultra* in the monastic life. The Carthusian vocation is the mystic peak, the Everest to which all aspire but few attain. The original way of life, in form and in spirit, remains unchanged, and fears that the Carthusians must adapt themselves to the modern world if they are to survive have proved groundless in post-war years, which have seen a resurgence which has made itself felt even across the Atlantic."[59] Although this resurgence, situated as it was in the mid-twentieth century, helps to contextualize the foundation of the Vermont Carthusians, the impact is also noteworthy. Indeed, as one author writing in 2006 explains regarding recent developments in membership in the Charterhouse of the Transfiguration: "The year 2003 was a year of rich blessings in terms of vocations. At the end of the fall of that year the community totaled sixteen: six cloister monks, six lay brothers, and four aspirants/postulants. In December 2006 there were six choir monks and eight lay brothers."[60] Perhaps public disclosure of Carthusian life and practice through the filming and showing of *Into Great Silence*, as well as websites, articles, and book publications about the Carthusian Order and the American Carthusians, in particular, may again be situated in the context of appeal to precedent. Despite their withdrawal and renunciation, the early desert fathers and their successors were engaged and involved in the world in all sorts of ways. Through many forms of controlled access, they bore witness to a means of being Christian and offered guidance and counsel to those seeking it. A relationship of mutual benefit, rooted in a form of patronage, was evident in these encounters. While it is certain that, unlike his fourth-century counterpart, the twenty-first century Carthusian monk requires the capacity to negotiate social relations of a different order and in a different time, it is the case that such negotiation must still occur. One form of this may be evident today in the patronage required for the creation and maintenance of a Carthusian monastery on American soil.

As we have seen, the structure of the Carthusian monastery and of the hermitage cell contributes directly to the vocation to be realized in these spaces as spaces embedded with meaning and value. The play of external form and internal function is a way of defining this meaning and value that can be seen in a variety of seeming juxtapositions. For example, in the

---

59. Edwards, *Worlds Apart*, 23.
60. See Schlegel and Hogg, *Monasticon Cartusiense*, 12.

relationship between anonymity and individuality, while the Carthusian monk is anonymous to those outside the monastery (recall, for example, that authorship is ascribed as "a Carthusian monk") he is recognized in a deeply personal, and intimate as an individual before God. In the relationship of permanence and impermanence, while there is stability in the structure of Carthusian life and practice and a reliance on the rhythmic routine of its discipline, there is a constant awareness of death and the impermanence of this life. In the relationship of silence and sound, while the silence of human speech grounds a central feature of Carthusian life and practice, it does not do so at the expense of sound as it heightens the opportunity for listening to the natural world in and around the monastery, to the bells that toll to mark transitions in the day, and to verbalized prayer and chant as forms of communication with the divine. Finally, in the relationship of solitude and community, the Carthusian expression and form, structured as it is in a community of hermits, is rooted in principles of charity, love, humility and mutual obedience. For those in the world, the Carthusian desert does, in many respects, serve as the desert of the ancient monks did, namely, as a counter-cultural site of ambiguity and encounter.[61]

Writing in the early period of the Carthusian presence in the United States, in his book *The Silent Life*, Thomas Merton observed:

> The Charterhouse in America will have to meet the great temptations which this country offers to all the monastic Orders: publicity, technology, popularity, commercialism, machines and the awful impulse to throw everything overboard for the sake of fame and prosperity (masking as an "apostolate of example"). One feels that the Carthusians are equipped, as no other Order, to resist this attack of the world upon the monastic spirit. The whole monastic structure in America may eventually depend on their doing so successfully.[62]

Nearly thirty years later, Merton's proposal remains prominent in the perspective of Robin Bruce Lockhart who, remarking on his visit to the Charterhouse of the Transfiguration, was careful to record that he observed "an even greater determination to maintain the Carthusian desert than I had observed elsewhere; a determination that under no circumstances

---

61. Jasper, *Sacred Desert*, 47, observes that: "The desert deconstructs and cleanses our categories of history and place and leads us physically to a space that is beyond the physical to the frustration of our quotidian earthly experience."

62. Merton, *Silent Life of the Carthusians*. Merton's *Silent Life* was originally published in 1957.

would the materialistic American way of life encroach upon the monks' seclusion."[63] Debating the value of making the Carthusian presence in the United States more widely known, Lockhart concludes: "The great paradox which overhangs Carthusian life in the United States is that, whereas more and more Americans are opening their hearts to the contemplative ideal, only the tiniest handful of the population can be aware of the Carthusian presence in its midst."[64] If accurate, Lockhart's observation and caution will require sustained negotiation.

The Vermont Carthusians joined the ranks of American Catholics during a period of intense self-definition. Over the course of their time in the United States, there is an unfailing persistence in their endeavor to perpetuate as unchanged the space and unwavering purpose of the monastery and the place of the hermitage cell. For this reason, their ability to continue to define and to negotiate their hiddenness on their own terms in order to serve as they believe they have been called may be *the most visible* witness of their lives and practice and in accordance with the *Statutes of the Carthusian Order*.[65]

---

63. Lockhart, *Halfway to Heaven*, 107.

64. Ibid., 108. Asking whether the Carthusians can live and flourish in the United States, a Cathusian monk, in *Carthusian Life and Its Inner Spirit*, 11, replies: "Seeing that the perfection of charity is a gift that God gives to all mankind, and not a special prerogative of any nation or type of character, there is no reason why there should not be a Charterhouse in the United States." In their hiddenness, in all of its dimensions, and in their anonymity, Carthusian monks strive to be (and are recognized as) invisible patrons through their imitation, witness and prayer.

65. *Statutes of the Carthusian Order* 4.34.2. See also the four-volume series, *Saint Bruno Pilgrim of the Absolute*, and in particular vol. 2 for pertinent and insightful considerations about being at the heart of the Church and of the relationship to the world and society.

4

Contemplation in Solitude
The Order of Cistercians of the Strict Observance

The human task, torn between freedom and grace, is the peaceful acceptance of a broken heart. It is a question of the emptiness or a void which is there to welcome nothing more than grace. If there is effort involved, it's that which belongs to human fragility perpetually confronted by its own limits.[1]

THE CISTERCIAN ABBEY OF OUR LADY OF THE HOLY TRINITY IS LOCATED in Huntsville, Utah. Resting on over two thousand acres, just north of Ogden and Salt Lake City, the monastery is nestled in a broad, fertile valley. It is accessible off a long main road. The monastery was founded in 1947 with the help of then local Bishop Hunt as a daughter house to the Cistercian Abbey of Gethsemani in the central part of Kentucky. The monastery is located in the heart of a strong Mormon population. Like Cistercian monasteries around the world, the Abbey of the Holy Trinity is self-sustaining. The nineteen monks who live there work together to maintain the vibrant life and work of the monastery. Manual labor typically has a strong agricultural focus in Cistercian practice, and the Abbey of the Holy Trinity is no exception. On sizeable, fertile fields the monks grow alfalfa and soybeans, raise black angus cattle, and are known nationwide for their honey production. Hospitality is exercised generously, and one of the buildings on the monastery grounds is set apart for the purposes of retreats by persons who come from all across the country.[2]

---

1. Louf, *Way of Humility*, 16.
2. For additional information, see the Holy Trinity Abbey website, http://holytrinityabbey.org.

Seeking in Solitude

The Order of Cistercians of the Strict Observance

The Order of Cistercians of the Strict Observance (also referred to as Trappist) traces its origins as a contemplative monastic order to the *Rule of St. Benedict*.[3] During the period of monastic reform of the eleventh century, Robert, abbot of the Benedictine monastery of Molesme, led a group of monks seeking stricter practice to an isolated region in Cîteaux where they cultivated a more rigorous application of the *Rule of St. Benedict* and a more austere ascetic discipline.[4] Under the direction of two successive abbots, Alberic and Stephen Harding, the monastery at Cîteaux was stabilized and grew.[5] During the twelfth century, St. Bernard of Clairvaux, a renowned member of the Order, served the Church of his day as both a prominent religious leader and a mystical theologian, and the Order continued to expand under his influence.[6] Further reforms to the Order

---

3. For a brief history of the Cistercian Order, see Perata, *Orchards of Perseverance*, 1–9. See also Berman, *Women and Monasticism in Medieval Europe*. Bokenhotter, *Concise History of the Catholic Church*, 132, writes: "A certain spiritual mediocrity began to manifest itself, and a new group of reformers arose within the order who were unhappy with the growing luxury."

4. Lekai, *Cistercians*, 23, writes after appraisal of scholarship on the manuscript tradition of central documents of the Order: "It remains true that the founders of Cîteaux intended to return to a stricter interpretation of the Rule. Their efforts resulted not in the restoration of the monastic life of the sixth century, but in the introduction of a life strongly influenced by the ideals of pre-Benedictine monasticism." This included efforts to live an eremitical life. See also Leclercq, *Love of Learning*, 99, for the sustained role of previous generations and figures in the history of monasticism: "In all controversies between monks, as for example when the Cluniacs are in opposition to Cistercians, each party appeals to St. Anthony and does so legitimately because what is remembered of his discourses is not the attacks against the Arians which were borrowed from him by St. Athanasius: what is recalled of his life is neither its historical circumstances nor the details of his temptations and the diabolic imagery with which the biographer had adorned it; it is rather the spiritual themes and instructions which are valid for all monks, regardless of the observance under which they lived." On this period of monastic reform, see Hutchison, *Hermit Monks of Grandmont*, 19, where Hutchison draws attention to the issue of numbers as a partial explanation for "why monks turned hermits in the eleventh century and reverted to their cenobitic state in the twelfth." See also Williams, "Early Cistercian Documents."

5. See Schaefer, "Earliest Churches of the Cistercian Order," 195–207.

6. On this period, see Berman, *Medieval Agriculture*, and Donkin, *Cistercians*. Organizational development occurred in this period as well. See Rorimer, *Cloisters*, xxv, who writes that "the influence of Cluny and Citeaux led to voluntary unions of houses observing the same rule; and in the thirteenth century the Benedictine abbeys in the various ecclesiastical provinces were required to form federations, called congregations."

initiated under Armand-Jean Bouthiellier de Rancé, the Abbot of the Monastery of La Trappe, in the seventeenth century, emphasized austerity and strict observance of ascetic discipline.[7] Decrees of expulsion by the French government in the late eighteenth century forced many of the monks to flee the country and to resettle in various monasteries throughout Europe.[8] Repopulation of the monasteries in France occurred after the demise of Napolean and, in 1892, the Order of Cistercians of the Strict Observance, having a contemplative focus, was defined and developed. Today, there are Trappist and Cistercian monasteries of common observance throughout the world, including several that may be found in various locations across the continental United States.

There are two items pertaining to those in the Order of Cistercians of the Strict Observance and those in the Sacred Order of Citeaux, which maintains what is referred to as the common observance that merit our further attention. First, members of both Orders are rooted in the *Rule of St. Benedict* and in the reforms instituted by Robert of Molesme and those monks who accompanied him. However, despite this shared foundation, there is an element of distinction evident between the Orders. Trappists, whose practices emerged from internal efforts to locate a place for an interpretation of the *Rule of St. Benedict*, the *Charter of Charity*, and the *Constitutions of the Monks* (2005) that enabled and then facilitated a more stringent cultivation of poverty and simplicity, are a particular group whose

---

7. On Armand-Jean Bouthiellier de Rancé and the reforms of this period, see Krailsheimer, *Rancé and the Trappist Legacy*, and Bell, *Understanding Rancé*. Lekai, *Rise of the Cistercian*, 3, observes: "Reforms, when studied in their historical settings, appear to be more or less conscious efforts to secure a safe place for an old religious body within a changed social and cultural environment. Such had been the case of the first Cistercian reform in the twelfth century and, though on a far more modest scale, such was the goal that animated the renewal of the Order in the seventeenth century." See also Knowles, *Christian Monasticism*, 162: "Rancé defies appraisal. Supremely self-confident and to all appearances either strangely obtuse or capable of complete self-deception, he nevertheless dies an abbot of zeal and a leader who inspired others to lives of spiritual heroism, and his work lived on to revivify the whole order." The monastery of La Trappe would remain a site for strict discipline and would survive during the French Revolution.

8. On this, see the discussion of Abbot Lestrange and his efforts to preserve the Order in this period in Lekai, *Cistercians*, 179–92. Consider also Gran, *Hand on My Shoulder*, 2:34: "But the monks were not so easily tricked. One night in 1791 they crossed the frontier to Switzerland where they were allowed to settle in a disused Carthusian monastery (Val-Sainte). Here the community experienced a revival and expansion that resulted in new foundations, not only in Europe but in Canada and the USA. After twenty-five years in exile, they succeeded in winning back their confiscated abbey. La Trappe survived excellently and still carries on."

place originates in the move toward a life of contemplation. Those Cistercians belonging to the Sacred Order of Citeaux, while also tracing their origins to the reforms of Robert of Molesme in the eleventh century, focused their work on the areas of parochial education and pastoral activity.[9]

In the face of many challenges, renewed efforts as well as a changed social and religious climate made it possible for several monasteries of the Order of Cistercians of the Strict Observance to be founded in the United States.[10] The Abbey of Gethsemani was founded in 1848, and the Abbey of New Melleray was founded near Dubuque, Iowa, in 1849.[11] Expansion occurred steadily through the founding of many more monasteries across the United States. Today, there are twelve male, and five female, monasteries in thirteen different states; these include the Abbey of Gethsemani and the Abbey of the Holy Trinity.[12] Although each monastery has distinctive features, Trappist monasteries share several distinguishing characteristics. In his work *Roman Catholicism in America*, Chester Gillis writes that each monastery is "home to a small community of monks who intersperse daily work on a farm, a printing press, or a workshop with times of solitude,

---

9. Monasteries of the Order of Citeaux in the United States are found in New Jersey (Cistercian Monastery) and in Pennsylvania (Monastery of St. Mary). For a listing, see Louf, *Cistercian Way*, 153–54.

10. Trappists are members of the contemplative Order of Cistercians of the Strict Observance (OCSO). See Patera, *Orchards of Perseverance*, 8: "On December 21, 1848, forty-five monks from Melleray founded the Abbey of Gethsemani, the first lasting Cistercian monastery in America." See also the discussion in Rippinger, *Benedictine Order in the United States*, 210–23. Observing the growth of the Order in the post-war period, Lekai, *Cistercians*, 210, writes that "in the United States alone, between 1944 and 1956, the number of Trappist establishments grew from three to twelve, while membership increased from about three hundred to one thousand." For discussion of the earlier efforts of Dom Urban Guillet, see Garraghan, "Trappists of Monks Mound," 94–135. On the founding of Gethsemani, see Raymond, *Burnt Out Incense*.

11. See Aprile, *Abbey of Gethsemani*. For the founding of the Abbey of New Melleray, see O'Connor, *New Melleray Abbey*.

12. This is a sizable presence in relation to the other forms of eremitic life and practice considered in this book. For a map of Trappist Abbeys in the United States, see the opening pages of Bianco, *Lives of the Trappists Today*. For a historical and comparative discussion of statistics and geographical distribution of male Cistercians across the world, see Dubois, "Order of Cistercians of the Strict Observance." For a historical and comparative discussion of statistics and geographical distribution of female Cistercians across the world, see Pini, "Order of Cistercians of the Strict Observance." There is a considerable body of source material on the Cistercian and Trappist ways of life. As well, there is a growing body of visitor accounts. In addition to sources previously cited, one might refer to Nouwen, *Genessee Diary*, and Sweeney, *Cloister Talks*.

prayer, and community living."[13] Self-sufficiency entails economic sustainability; some Trappist monasteries sell a range of goods. As indicated earlier, the Abbey of the Holy Trinity produces honey, among other items. Other Trappist monasteries produce other goods including, for example, eggs, compost, and jams, in order to provide or supplement income.[14]

The Order of Cistercians of the Strict Observance is a monastic religious order guided by the *Rule of St. Benedict*,[15] the *Charter of Charity*,[16] and the *Constitutions of the Monks*.[17] The cenobitic, or communal, life of the monks is overseen by an abbot[18] and all monks take vows of obedience, stability and conversion of manners.[19] Each monastery is independent, and all monasteries are bound by a bond of charity to the other monasteries of the Order across the world.[20] According to the *Constitutions of the Monks*, each monk is called to withdraw from the world and to dwell in the desert through a life of solitude, silence, and self-denial, cultivating humility, obedience, and simplicity, in prayer, manual labor and hospitality.[21] In accordance with the *Rule of St. Benedict*, the daily *horarium* of Cistercian monks

---

13. Gillis, *Roman Catholicism in America*, 174.

14. Information about goods produced at Trappist monasteries is often available at an individual monastery's book or gift shop, or website. Some local businesses stock these products, as well.

15. See de Vogüé, "Rule of Saint Benedict." For an interesting discussion regarding the relationship of the religious to the monastic life in the early formulation of the Code of Canon Law, see Truyen, "Are Monks Religious?" On the significance of the religious life as a fraternal life in the New Code of Canon Law, see Louf, "Living in Community."

16. The *Charter of Charity* (*Summa Carta Caritatis*, 1119 CE) was issued under Abbot Stephen Harding and marks distinctive features of Cistercian organization and governance. See Nigg, *Warriors of God*, 210, who explains that according to the *Charter of Charity* "the individual houses are encouraged to pursue their independent development under a freely elected abbot who is no mere prior subject to Citeaux but who enjoys all the rights of his office. At the same time, all the abbots must undertake to follow Citeaux in the interpretation of the rule." See also Knowles, *Christian Monasticism*, 75, who writes that "two safeguards unknown to contemporary monarchism were imposed." These "safeguards" included a system of visitation and the annual general chapter.

17. For the *Constitutions of the Monks* (2005), see http://www.ocso.org/index.php?option=com_docman&Itemid=122&lang=en.

18. *Constitutions of the Monks* (2005), I.C.3.1.

19. Ibid., II.1.C. 9, C.10, and C.11.

20. Ibid., I.C.4.1. Filiation is operative in the Cistercian Order. See Constitution 4.2 which makes reference to the role of this document, and of the *Charter of Charity* in the governance of the Order.

21. Ibid., I.C.3.3.

offers balanced periods of work and prayer, and balanced opportunities for fellowship in community and for individual contemplation. An emphasis on poverty and simplicity is pervasive, as these remain vestigial elements of reform that are still defining features.[22] In his assessment of the "Cistercian revolution," monastic author David Knowles writes that these elements were fundamental to the reform of the eleventh century. He observes that the Cistercians, "by shearing off almost all the liturgical accretions save for the Mass, and by simplifying the chant and ceremonial, restored work and reading and private prayer to their earlier position as partners of the *Opus Dei*."[23] In these terms, reform was a return to a previous interpretation and emphasis; reform was a means by which select persons were able to revive and embody these elements once more present and prominent in monastic life and practice. These are elements that remain embedded in Cistercian life and practice today.

Hospitality remains an important form of relationship between the monastery and outsiders. Hospitality contributes to the preservation of a balance between community and contemplation, the mundane and the loftier, the cloister and the world. According to the *Rule of St. Benedict*, monks are instructed to receive guests graciously because of the example of Christ as indicated in *Rule* 53, "The Reception of Guests," which begins, "All guests who present themselves are to be received in spirit as Christ would be received, for he himself will say: I was a stranger and you welcomed me. Proper honor must be shown to all, especially to those who share our faith and to pilgrims."[24] Guidelines for the satisfaction of a guest's physical, social, and spiritual needs are also found in the *Rule* where hospitality was "surrounded by ritual and carefully circumscribed interaction."[25] Again, *Rule* 53 provides clear parameters and emphasizes that encounter

---

22. Olivera, "Monastic Vision," xiv, has described Cistercian life in these terms: "Among the exercises practiced yesterday, today, and always, the following should be listed: silent and continual prayer, liturgical prayer centered in the Eucharist, *lectio divina*, the asceticism of fasting, Vigils, work, voluntary poverty, and the different renunciations (chastity and obedience) leading to the heart's conversion and purification, with everything lived in a climate of solitude and silence." See also Belisle, *Language of Silence*, 105–13. For an example of a Trappist *horarium*, see Knowles, *Christian Monasticism*, 197–98.

23. Knowles, *Christian Monasticism*, 221.

24. Fry, trans., *Rule of St. Benedict*, 51.

25. Pohl, *Making Room*, 47. Clearly hospitality has many ends including contact with those outside the cloister, the reception of alms and other forms of intercession including prayer.

with a guest, with an "other," in the act of hospitality reflects the Christian call for solidarity through service issued in the gospels. There are separate rules, including *Rule* 61, dedicated to the reception of visiting monks[26] and, likewise, other rules such as *Rule* 58 for those who come to the monastery with the specific intention of seeking admission to the monastic life.[27] The *Rule of St. Benedict* also provides additional guidelines for those monks whose tasks will bring them necessarily into contact with a guest.[28] In the *Rule of St. Benedict*, hospitality is a vital component of the monastic vocation. As part of "the Lord's service,"[29] it is rooted in scriptural mandate and connected to conceptions of divine judgment. Benedictine hospitality is governed by explicit guidelines for acceptable behavior and interaction between guest and host in order to prevent disruptiveness and to preserve stability. In this context, hospitality is characterized by love, humility, reception, prayer, instruction, and kindness.

The post-conciliar impact of Vatican Council II's call to monastic renewal was a significant moment in the history and definition of the Cistercian Order.[30] As a result of the council's call to renewal, Michael Casey, OCSO, writes that there appears to be a shift "away from concentration on the minutiae of external observance in the direction of greater pluralism, on the understanding that fundamental beliefs and values have been internalized."[31] Father Casey suggests that the relationship between external discipline and personal formation may continue to thrive in the future. He writes: "It is by personally appropriating the wisdom of the past that future generations will develop the capacity to interact creatively with their own period."[32] Father Casey and others have maintained that the contemplative focus of the Order of the Cistercians of the Strict Observance will be

---

26. Fry, trans., *Rule of St. Benedict*, 59.

27. Ibid., 56.

28. Ibid., 31, 35.

29. Ibid., prologue.

30. See "Declaration on Cistercian Life by the 1969 General Chapter of the Order of Cistercians of the Strict Observance" and "Statute on Unity and Pluralism of the 1969 General Chapter O.C.S.O.," 149–52. Both documents include contemplation, fundamental observances of the Order, and shared values as defining features.

31. Casey, "Thoughts on Monasticism's Possible Futures," 27. For a perspective on renewal at the time of the call, see Johnson, "Charter of Charity." One might pair this with the perspective later offered by Conchuir, "Diminishing Communities."

32. Ibid.

essential to its place in the Church and in the world in the future.[33] Among those who have written about the place of contemplative life in the future is Abbot André Louf who also draws attention to this focus and observes that, "Above all there has been an attempt to restore the formative power of the monastic life itself for the monk. The ancient fathers had always been aware of this and had believed in it. But if the life itself is to form the monk and to teach him the ways of God, then it must be adapted patiently and pliably to the work of grace in each one, and to the potential of each individual."[34] The *Constitutions of the Monks* (2005) provide teaching on monastic formation and the form of monastic life, especially evident in teaching about the communal and eremitic forms of practice that will be particularly attentive to assuring that the individual monk is embracing the life to which he is called.

As we have seen, as a member of a cenobitic order, the Cistercian monk is bound by several vows.[35] Among these is a vow of stability. Stability has several dimensions in the context of Cistercian life among which is included stability of place; the monk vows to dedicate his life to Cistercian monastic practice in a particular monastic community.[36] The monk's identity is thus shaped by, and contributes to the shaping of, the specific community of which he is a member. The monk's vow of stability is a lifelong commitment, as Cistercians monks are buried in a cemetery on the grounds of their monastery. Moreover, stability of place requires that the monk be given permission by the abbot to leave the monastery.[37]

---

33. Ibid., 28. The significance of the contemplative orientation is found as well in the 1969 Statute on Unity and Pluralism. See also Bamberger, "Fragments for a Vision of Cistercian Life."

34. Louf, *Cistercian Way*, 43. See also the insights of Spreafico, "Community, Subject of Evangelization (I)," 352, who writes with regard to monasteries in the mission of the Church: "It is not a question of adaptation to the spirit of the times but of a living interpretation of the Tradition under the guidance of the Holy Spirit, and thus it becomes a prophetic witness going against the spirit of the times."

35. Professed vows can be found Rule 58, "Regulations Regarding the Admission of Brothers," in *Rule of St. Benedict*.

36. See *Constitutions of the Monks* (2005), II.1.C.9.

37. Ibid., II.1.C.13.3.

Eremitic Life and Practice in the Cistercian Order of the Strict Observance, OCSO

This is especially relevant for the interpretation of the eremitic life and practice in the context of the Cistercian Order of the Strict Observance.[38] The *Constitutions of the Monks* (2005) specifically addresses the eremitical life in two different sections. In each section, the eremitical life is discussed alongside other situations in which the monk may reside outside the monastery. The first mention of the eremitical life is found in Constitution 13.3.[39] According to this Constitution, permission of the abbot and his council is required for a monk to live outside the monastery in order to live the eremitical life.[40] The wording of the Constitution implies that the eremitical life may not always be lived in a hermitage on the monastery grounds, since the additional permission of the local bishop is required if the hermit resides in a location that is off the property of the monastery.[41] Regardless of location, the hermit continues to cultivate the vow of obedience to the *Rule of St. Benedict*, to the *Constitutions of the Monks* (2005), and the authority of the abbot.[42] In addition to the eremitical life, prolonged absence from the monastery, of a period longer than one year, may be allowed for reasons of health, in cases whereby a monk requires the treatment of an illness, or of further study.[43]

---

38. See Schaefer, "Earliest Churches of the Cistercian Order," 195–207. Schaefer draws on the results of the work of several scholars, including Jean Leclercq and Louis Lekai, who have examined the eremitic lives and practices of the early founders of the Cistercian Order. For discussion of hermitage, wilderness, and desert in the context of the foundation at Cîteaux, see Farkasfalvy, "Biblical Vocabulary," 156–57.

39. *Constitutions of the Monks* (2005), pt. II, ch. 1, Constitution 13.3 is among those that were modified by the Meeting of the General Chapters in 2005. The concluding statement of Constitution 13.3 (unmodified) identifies the eremitical life as an extraordinary case under which a monk may live outside the monastery. The modification to Constitution 13.3 that was approved at this Meeting addresses, in a specific way, the means by which the decision to lead the eremitical life is made, the parameters of obedience, and the location of practice. This modification is defined as Statute 13.3.A.

40. See *Constitutions of the Monks* (2005), II.1.C.13.3.

41. Ibid. So, e.g., the Cistercian Abbey of the Holy Trinity in Huntsville, UT, has a hermitage on the grounds of the monastery that is removed (about 40 minutes walking distance) from the central location of the monastery.

42. Ibid. See also Dubois, "Authority and Obedience," for a discussion of obedience in connection to the authority of the *Rule of St. Benedict* and to the abbot.

43. Ibid.

Seeking in Solitude

The second mention of the eremitical life is found in Constitution 36.3.[44] This Constitution assures that those who are absent from the monastery keep their place in the conventual chapter, which consists of all those members who have professed permanent vows.[45] Here, again, the Constitution applies not only to hermits, but to those who may be absent for other reasons including service to the monastery, health, or study.[46] Whereas the earlier Constitution 13.3 addresses the location of the eremitic practice in relation to the space of the monastery, the later Constitution 36.3 articulates the role of the hermit in relation to the community of monks to which he is bound.

As we have seen, in several cases the *Constitutions of the Order* make clear that Cistercian solitude and silence may be interpreted in and through the eremitic form of practice. Following the foundation of the Cistercian Order of the Strict Observance in the United States, the eremitic practice has been, and continues to be, adopted. Evidence is found across foundations.[47] In accordance with the first rule of the *Rule of St. Benedict*, these hermits are among those "who have been well trained by a lengthy period of probation in the monastery with the support of many others and have learned to fight against the devil."[48] Dwelling on the grounds of their monasteries in hermitage sites, they live in further solitude and separation bound to the members of their community through common vows and a life of prayer and contemplation.

For these Cistercian monks, further removal and withdrawal from the monastery to the hermitage site for the more solitary cultivation of silence and solitude is not a dismissal of the role of the community; rather, as practitioners and monastic scholars have maintained, the eremitic practice is an affirmation that the cultivation of solitude and silence remain defined and located in the context of the Cistercian community.[49] For example, as one

44. See *Constitutions of the Monks* (2005), II.2.C.36.3, Statute 36.3.A.

45. Ibid.

46. Ibid.

47. Among those members of the Cistercian Order of the Strict Observance in the United States who are known through their writings are Father John Eudes Bamberger (Abbey of the Genesee) and Father Thomas Merton (Gethsemani Monastery in Trappist, Kentucky). Another widely published member who lived and practiced outside of the United States, in a hermitage in southern France, was Dom André Louf.

48. White, trans., *Rule of St. Benedict*, 11.

49. Affirmation that solitude and silence remains situated in the context of the Cistercian community is found, e.g., in Downey, *Trappist*. It is also affirmed in Teahan, "Solitude."

scholar, John D. Barbour, writes in his study of solitude, for the Cistercian monk, hermit, and author, Father Thomas Merton, solitude and community were, "at least in principle, mutually dependent rather than antagonistic."[50] Barbour explains that, "A hermit needs the continuing support of a community, both in material ways and for an occasional reality check, to prevent delusion, and to seek guidance. A community shows its integrity and respect for personhood when it values and nurtures solitaries."[51] The suggested mutuality in the relationship between solitude and community indicates that, in the context of Cistercian life and practice, solitude and silence are extended to the location of the hermitage in a way that permits the deeper cultivation of each without loss, or compromise, of either. The sustained connection of the hermit to the community and of the community to the hermit that is defined in the *Constitutions of the Monks* (2005) further assures that solitude and silence are lived as distinctively Cistercian ideals, and so contribute to the collaborative life of contemplation and effort expressly articulated in the *Rule of St. Benedict* "to establish a school for the Lord's service."[52]

The particular relationship between cenobitic and eremitic elements in Trappist life and practice appears to uphold core values of silence and simplicity; it provides a balanced life of work and prayer; it is rooted in contemplation. The monastery space is structured to accommodate and frame these elements; hermitage sites are included as an important form of life and practice, and they provide space for more solitary, eremitic practice.

Solitude and Silence as a Form of Cistercian Presence in the United States

In the opening paragraph of his article "Solitude: A Central Motif in Thomas Merton's Life and Writings," author John Teahan observes that "monasticism and mysticism in their most profound forms manifest something far more interesting than the literal practice of silence and solitude: monks and mystics often understand solitude as the climate and silence as

---

50. Barbour, *Value of Solitude*, 170.

51. Ibid. Here Barbour's explanation is in the context of a statement about the relationship between solitude and community in Thomas Merton's *Thoughts in Solitude*. For discussion of the development of Thomas Merton's thought on solitude, see also Lentfoehr, "Solitary," 59–78.

52. White, trans., *Rule of St. Benedict*, prologue.

Seeking in Solitude

the language of liberation, enlightenment, or union with God. Silence and solitude then become sacred metaphors, often more than metaphors, to express the experience of ultimate transformation."[53] Teahan's observation highlights the interdependence between silence and solitude in a way that upholds the distinctiveness and respective role of each in "the experience of ultimate transformation." Furthermore, his observation may offer a useful framework for considering how solitude and silence exist and operate in relationship in the specific context of Cistercian life and practice and, in this, to one of the ways in which the external form of monastic life and practice contributes to the attainment of an internal focus and aim.[54]

Cultivated in the context of the monastery or in the hermitage, solitude and silence are foundational elements of Cistercian life and practice. Michael Downey, author of *Trappist: Living in the Land of Desire*, writes that "Trappist life is life in community, but a community of a distinct kind in which the brothers are brought together and sustained by a bond of solitude and of silence."[55] Solitude and silence have a structural framework that is evident in several external, exterior forms. The geographical location of a Cistercian monastery, the layout of the monastic site, the architecture of the monastery church, and the prescriptions of the *Rule of St. Benedict* are some of the ways that solitude is created. Through the construction of enclosure, the definition of self-sufficiency, the cultivation of a community of contemplation, and adherence to the guiding framework of the daily *horarium*, solitude is an essential component of the framework and orientation of Cistercian monastic life and practice. It is in this structure that the cultivation of silence may be situated and understood.

Through physical solitude, visible in the location and foundation of Cistercian monasteries, the Cistercian monk is removed from society.[56] In his work *The Monastic Achievement*, George Zarnecki writes that physical withdrawal was an explicit outcome of the Cistercian reform. "The ascetic aims of the founders demanded that the monks should live as far away as

---

53. Teahan, "Solitude," 521. Teahan's article contributes specifically to his work on these features in the life of Thomas Merton. I hope here to suggest that Teahan's observation is applicable to the broader context of several features of Cistercian life (and, indeed, the observation could be applied to a consideration of other non-Cistercian contemplative monastic contexts).

54. This internal aim and focus may be considered by appeal to Martin, "Cistercian Monasticism and Modern Adaptations." See also Pollard and Davis, "Monastic Solitude."

55. Downey, *Trappist*, 108.

56. See Louf, "Apostolic and Contemplative Dimension of Religious Life."

possible from the centres of wealth and power. The abbeys were to be built far from cities and settlements and the monks and lay brothers were themselves to cultivate the land."[57] This initial intent has been preserved as the locations of Cistercian monasteries remain removed, though not wholly inaccessible, from the public sphere. In the United States, Cistercian monasteries are typically found on large acreages of land that can be cultivated through labor and appreciated for the natural beauty that surrounds them.[58]

This initial intent for, and interpretation of, solitude has also been preserved in the architecture and design of a Cistercian monastery. Here, too, as John W. Cook and Allan Doig explain, "The rigorous asceticism of the Cistercian monastic rule and life was directly reflected in their architecture."[59] A Cistercian monastery has a clearly defined arrangement and a style that Louis J. Lekai refers to as "characteristically Cistercian."[60] Moreover, a Cistercian monastery is intended to be a self-sufficient community. A typical Cistercian monastery of the medieval period contained several buildings that were structured around a central or main cloister and garden. Surrounding monastery buildings included the monastery church, the kitchen and refectory, and the dormitory. Keeping in mind that agriculture was an important form of manual labor, additional buildings were set apart to accommodate stables, workshops, and storage facilities for equipment. Today, these basic structural elements are also present in Cistercian monasteries in the United States.[61]

In addition to geographic location and internal structure, the Cistercian monastery church is another way in which we might consider the meaning of solitude. The layout of a Cistercian monastery is structured so that it features the church as the primary building. Cistercian churches emphasize the values of poverty and simplicity; they give attention to

---

57. Zarnecki, *Monastic Achievement*, 70.

58. Nature plays an important role in Cistercian thought and theology. For the relationship between the hours of the Divine Office in Cistercian practice and the movement of the sun, see Freeman, *Come and See*, 184. A description of the Cistercian day can be found in Louf, *Cistercian Way*, 46–49.

59. Cook and Doig, "Architecture," *Encyclopedia of Christianity*, 59.

60. Lekai, *Cistercians*, 264. For Cistercian architecture, see Brown, *God and Enchantment of Place*, 270–71.

61. Those unable to visit a Cistercian monastery can see these elements in two documentaries: *Vina* (1973), about the Abbey of New Clairvaux in California; and *Trappist* (2008), about Mepkin Abbey in South Carolina. See also Brown, *God and Enchantment of Place*.

building materials and workmanship; they are forums for contemplation and so highlight light, natural beauty and open space.[62] These features are prominent in several contemporary descriptions of Cistercian churches. Consider this description of the church that is part of Mepkin Abbey in South Carolina. The description is contained in *Trappist*, a book about daily life at the monastery. "The building is almost barnlike in its utter simplicity; it is light and airy. In part this is because of its many glass doors, a rarity in a monastic church. The vaulted ceiling made of southern yellow pine beams adds height and grace to the building, endowing it with extraordinary acoustical properties . . . The Abbey Church at Mepkin invites the enjoyment of contemplative moments, indeed of prolonged contemplative experience, in and through the beauty of the building itself. It is sheer poetry in light; penetrating light plays with the simple, stark, and spare."[63] In the documentary film that accompanies this book, former Abbot Francis Kline, OCSO, explains the significance of the theological symbolism of light in the Cistercian tradition, drawing on the work of St. Bernard of Clairvaux.[64] In both of these descriptions, the intentional ordering of the church space as an invitation for the infusion of natural light, is noteworthy. The Cistercian church is constructed to enable light to filter into and permeate the space of the church, illuminating it throughout. Attention to the natural role of light extends beyond the space of the church. That is, the connection to what occurs within the church and the natural world outside the church contributes, in a deeply meaningful, way as well to the experience of encounter and contemplation facilitated by the church space. In "Cistercian Grace

---

62. For an overview of the historiography of Cistercian architecture that includes attention to the issue of distinctiveness, see Fergusson, "Cistercian Architecture." Fergusson provides an engaging overview of some of the key issues and questions that have framed scholarship on Cistercian architecture by giving attention to the contributions of archeological excavations as well as interdisciplinary approaches; he includes focused treatment of whether there are Bernardine features in Cistercian architecture, introduced through the influence of Bernard of Clairvaux, and the question of whether there are distinctive Cistercian features after filiation. See also Dimier, *Stones before the Lord*. For earliest architectural forms, see Schaefer, "Earliest Churches of the Cistercian Order," 195–207.

63. Downey, *Trappist*, 60. See also Louf, *Cistercian Way*, 57, who describes the Cistercian church in these terms: "A bare church does away with distractions and draws the attention to God alone. The careful blending of light and shade, the use of authentic materials, and an emphasis on sobriety of line will achieve this. Poverty demands neither bad taste nor ugliness."

64. For an introduction to the mystical theology of St. Bernard of Clairvaux, see Evans, *Bernard of Clairvaux*.

Contemplation in Solitude

Today: Conformity to Christ," Abbot Joseph Boyle describes this relationship to the natural world in his Cistercian monastery church in Snowmass, Colorado in these terms: "Our singing is sometimes accompanied by the singing of the coyotes outside and our chapel's clear glass windows let in the grandeur of and beauty of the nature surrounding us."[65]

Here, again, there is theological and anthropological significance for the identity of the Cistercian monastic life.[66] As former Abbot Francis Kline, OCSO, explains, the monastic Church, like the monastery in which it resides, is a place of hope. He writes, "The monastic Church is called apart from all other gifts and missions of the Church, so that this light of Christ which it guards, proclaims, and lives by, may guide the Church on its way of return through all its manifold activities."[67] This characterization of the monastic Church proposes a vision of stability and constancy; looking toward the future, the monastic Church has a prophetic place and role in the present.

This brief consideration of the geographic location of the monastery, the layout of the Cistercian monastery, and the structure and design of the monastery church, in particular, help to frame the separation that is fundamental to the cultivation of silence in the context of Cistercian life and practice. The relationship between solitude and silence is widely discussed in literature about Cistercian life and practice. One statement about this relationship is found in *The Cistercian Way*, where Andre Louf, OCSO, writes, "In a life where everything is done in common, silence is essential if solitude is to be maintained."[68] This statement hearkens to the way in which silence enables a form of solitude that is cultivated in the context of community, in the context of being and living with others. Silence is a way of exercising solitude; it is a defining feature of how solitude is known and lived.

As a result, silence assumes a variety of expressions in Cistercian life and practice.[69] We have seen that monastic withdrawal is not only an expression of physical removal from urban life but a means of creating a

---

65. Boyle, "Cistercian Grace Today," 279.

66. Here we might consider the insight of Bamberger, "Fragments for a Vision," 144, who writes: "My view of Cistercian life then, in brief, is that it is ordered to the glory of God by offering him the best service possible: the recovery of the likeness to the Word of God through whom the whole cosmos is created."

67. Kline, "To What Holiness?," 182.

68. Louf, *Cistercian Way*, 124. See also Fitzpatrick, "Enclosure."

69. See Kline, "To What Holiness?"

space that is distinctly defined by the communal values and practices that shape Cistercian life. In this space, the cultivation of silence, manifest in a variety of forms, has the obvious aim of separating Cistercian monks from others and the possibly less visible aim of defining the community as a contemplative one. It also has the aim of defining the solitude essential for each individual monk in the community. As is the case with other forms of Cistercian life and practice, here too, the *Rule of St. Benedict* serves as the foundation for interpretation. Within the context of the Cistercian monastery, St. Benedict's teaching is interpreted and embedded in daily life and practice. For example, with regard to the practice of silence, the *Rule of St. Benedict* contains teaching that can be applied to the quantitative and qualitative aspects of speech. The sixth rule, in particular, "Restraint of Speech," appeals to Psalm 39:1–2, from which Benedict advises, "Here the prophet shows that if it is occasionally right to refrain from saying good things because one values silence, there is all the more reason to refrain from saying bad things because sin will be punished."[70] Guided in a life rooted in contemplation, in watchfulness and listening, the monk and the community are thus instructed in a way that not only restricts the use of speech but that does so in order to facilitate observation and discernment.

Obedience to the *Rule of St. Benedict* serves as a foundational source for the Cistercian cultivation of silence. Interpretation and implementation of silence is found, as well, in the more contemporary document, *Constitutions of the Monks* (2005). Constitution 24 states:

> Silence is counted among the principal monastic values of the Order. It assures solitude for the monk in community. It fosters mindfulness of God and fraternal communion. It opens the mind to the inspirations of the Holy Spirit and favours attentiveness of heart and solitary prayer to God. Therefore, at all times but especially during the hours of night, the brothers are to be zealous for silence, which is the guardian both of speech and of thought.[71]

The explicit connection between silence, speech, and thought emphasizes the significance of their place in the cultivation of solitude. Two other statutes that accompany this Constitution offer further qualification and explanation regarding the definition and application of silence. The first of these, Statute 24.A, draws attention to those places within the monastery where silence is especially upheld. These include the monastery church,

---

70. White, *Rule of St. Benedict*, 21.
71. See *Constitutions of the Monks* (2005), II.1.C. 24.

the refectory, and the scriptorium.[72] The second, Statute 24.B, gives each community the freedom to establish additional guidelines regarding the use of speech.[73]

Given these guidelines, we might also take a moment to consider the ways in which silence is cultivated during specific periods of the daily *horarium* which prescribe it. These periods are found throughout the daily *horarium* and preserve a balanced structure of individual and communal expressions.[74] Periods of silence draw focused attention to the use of speech as a form of oral communication within the community. These periods heighten awareness and enable sensitivity to the role of language as a means of contributing to the particular definition of monastic life in a Cistercian context. In this way, silence shapes the community and serves as the foundation for the way communication occurs between the monks. It also serves as an essential element in the formation and life of the individual monk. These communal and individual ends are emphasized in the "Statute on Unity and Pluralism of the 1969 General Chapter O.C.S.O." which addresses silence in these terms: "This search for a life of prayer should be lived in an atmosphere of recollection and silence for which all are responsible. In particular, the great silence at night and the silence in the regular places will be maintained."[75] For the individual monk, and for the community of monks, then, the physical act of silence as lack of speech is directly coupled with an ability of the heart to listen. The intentional connection between the sensory acts of speaking and hearing is a product of the transformative dimension of Cistercian life and practice. In this way, the restrictions on speech contribute to the orientation of the individual monk and of the monastic community toward contemplation, toward active listening to the Word of God, and toward a life of work and prayer. As Michael Downey, author of *Trappist: Living in the Land of Desire*, explains, "Silence is a tone of being. It is a disposition of hospitality to the Word of God. The monk's life is ordered to hearing the Word, receiving it, guarding it, keeping it."[76] Hospitality, here embodied as a form of hearing, further

---

72. See *Constitutions of the Monks* (2005), II.1.C.24, Statute 24.A.

73. See *Constitutions of the Monks* (2005), II.1.C.24, Statute 24.B. The application of this latter statute is clear in a retreat talk on silence by Freeman, *Come and See*, 86–87.

74. See Novices of Mont-des-Cats, "Grace and Law of Silence," 187–88.

75. Louf, *Cistercian Way*, 152.

76. Downey, *Trappist*, 90.

enables awareness and a receptivity that is distinctively cultivated in Cistercian monastic and eremitic practices.

Contemplative Solitude

In a 1968 article that appeared in *Cistercian Studies*, titled "The Christian Contemplative Community," author Sr. Myriam Dardenne writes that "the most radical solitude-if such a thing exists-is nourished by man and the world; solitude throws one back on one's fellowmen and on the One who opens for us the depth of all reality, Christ."[77] Given our consideration of Cistercian life and practice in this chapter, Sr. Dardenne's insight about solitude may be as pertinent to an understanding of this particular monastic and eremitic form today as it was nearly five decades ago.

---

77. Dardenne, "Christian Contemplative Community," 336.

5

A Listening Presence

The Hermits of Bethlehem in the Heart of Jesus

> Blessed is the one who bears the Cross and resurrection in one's heart, as well as the place of the Birth and Ascension of Christ. Blessed is the one who possesses Bethlehem in one's heart and in whose heart Christ is born daily.[1]

You can pick up Route 206, the state highway that runs along the eastern border of New Jersey, just a few miles outside Trenton, the state capital. Driving north upstate on Route 206 is a visual tale of settlement in the region. Swaths of unsettled, forested land dot much of the drive. Speed limits increase and then decrease sharply as you pass through the towns of Princeton, Bridgewater, and Bedminster. On a clear, hot June morning the traffic moves steadily slowing only for those few sections of the road under construction. If you are not careful and observant, you might miss the turn from the highway about forty miles later onto Furnace Road in the town of Chester. Passing through a well-kept residential area, you can then turn onto Pleasant Hill Road where, about a half a mile later, there are two signs. The further you drive down the long gravel access road following the sign for the Hermits of Bethlehem, the quieter it seems to get, and you immediately notice that you are passing through a densely wooded area that ends at an entrance gate and another driveway leading into the hermitage site. From the gate, you can see the simple wooden structures on the unenclosed space. In size and design, they are in sharp contrast to the homes on the

---

1. Romano, *A Way of Desert Spirituality: The Plan of Life of the Hermits of Bethlehem*, 105. Henceforward this will be referred to as *Plan of Life of the Hermits of Bethlehem*. The passage cited is from St. Jerome, Treatise on Psalm 95.

main road; suggesting simplicity and austerity, they reflect the purpose of the lives lived in this space.

Canonical Considerations: Canon 603 of the Revised Code of Canon Law

The Hermits of Bethlehem are a Laura of Consecrated Hermits of Diocesan Rite.[2] Their status as consecrated hermits is noteworthy given that canonical recognition of the eremitic vocation was awarded only very recently in the history of the Roman Catholic church in 1983, in Canon 603 of the *Revised Code of Canon Law*.[3] Within fourteen years of the *Revised Code*, the Hermits of Bethlehem were officially recognized as consecrated hermits; they were canonically erected on the Feast of the Immaculate Conception, on December 8, 1997.

The canons that address consecrated hermits, also referred to here as canonical hermits, in the *Revised Code of Canon Law* are found in the section focused on the institutes of consecrated life.[4] The opening canons of this section treat those who live the consecrated life in religious or secular institutes. Consecrated life in these institutes will later be differentiated from the consecrated life of the canonical hermit as defined by Canon 603 and so bear some attention here. In a religious institute "members pronounce

---

2. In this capacity as a form of consecrated life the Hermits of Bethlehem are connected closely to their local diocese.

3. A survey of diocesan activity with regard to recent developments on the consecrated life, including Canon 603, was conducted in spring 1993. The results are found in McDermott, "Recent Developments on Issues of Religious Law," 1–9. Although dated, the results and analysis published in this report remain useful as they provide an indication of the impact of Canon 603.

4. For discussion of the elements of institutes of consecrated life, see Caparros, Theriault, and Thom, *Code of Canon Law Annotated*, 411, where the editors note that the state of those in the consecrated life belongs "to the life and sanctity of the Church. It is a stable way of living the evangelical counsels which are a divine gift that the Church received from its Lord and which, with His grace, she conserves always, as Vatican II emphasized (cf. *Lumen Gentium* 43). This is why the Church orders all the faithful to foster and promote this special and stable form of life, although only certain persons will receive the special vocation required to live it." See also Cody, "New Canons on Consecrated Life," 64–68. See also Green, "Revised Code of Canon Law," 617, who writes: "Both the conciliar enterprise and the Code revision process were motivated by a profound concern to renew Christian life in the mid- and late- twentieth century. Furthermore, John Paul II viewed the revised Code as a noteworthy effort to translate the richness of conciliar doctrine into canonical language-however difficult, if not impossible, such a task is."

A Listening Presence

public vows, either perpetual or temporary which are to be renewed, however, when the period of time has elapsed, and lead a life of brothers or sisters in common."[5] The Camaldolese and Carthusians, whose eremitic practices were presented and discussed in earlier chapters, are examples of consecrated life in two different religious institutes. Unlike religious institutes, secular institutes are those "in which the Christian faithful, living in the world, strive for the perfection of charity and seek to contribute to the sanctification of the world, especially from within."[6] Those living the consecrated life in secular institutes, such as the Institute of the Heart of Jesus or the Secular Institute of St. Francis de Sales, both in the United States, are connected to the world in a way that is different from those in religious institutes.[7]

Canons about the three evangelical counsels of chastity, poverty, and obedience follow treatment of the consecrated life of those in religious and secular institutes. Each evangelical counsel is presented separately, and a statement regarding the fraternal union created by the profession of the evangelical counsels in the context of these institutes is also provided.[8]

Canon 603, addressing the consecrated life of the canonical hermit, appears after these canons. Several scholars have observed that the placement of the Canon 603 is noteworthy. Lived outside the framework of a religious or secular institute, and therefore not governed by the rules and laws of a respective institute, Canon 603 addresses a separate and distinct form of consecrated life in the eremitic vocation. As one commentator writes, Canon 603 formally recognizes that "hermits or anchorites represent one of the oldest forms of consecrated life in the history of the Church."[9] Given the

---

5. See *Code of Canon Law*, Canon 607.2, at http://www.vatican.va/archive/ENG1104/__P1Z.HTM.

6. See *Code of Canon Law*, Canon 710, at http://www.vatican.va/archive/ENG1104/__P2F.HTM.

7. See the information and directory found at the United States Conference of Secular Institutes website, http://www.secularinstitutes.org.

8. See Beal et al., *New Commentary on the Code of Canon Law*, 767, who write that Canon 603 "does not address the eremitical lifestyle provided for in the proper law of some religious institutes such as the Carthusians, Camaldolese, and Carmelites. Professed members of these institutes live as hermits under obedience to their legitimate superiors in accord with their proper law. Rather, it addresses solitary men or women living under the authority of a diocesan bishop."

9. The Canon Law Society of Great Britain and Ireland, *Canon Law Letter & Spirit*, 331. See Coriden et al., *Code of Canon Law*, 467, who observe that such placement is a shift from the 1977 schema of the revised law where "the canon explicitly dealing with

distinctive place of this form of eremitic life, Canon 603 supplies a definition for the life of the consecrated hermit as well as guidelines for the acquisition of this newly erected canonical status. Canon 603 is divided into two parts, or paragraphs; both paragraphs present distinguishing features in a succinct manner.

According to Canon 603.1 the distinctive and differentiating features of the consecrated hermit as a juridically recognized form of consecrated life are "a stricter separation from the world, the silence of solitude, and a life of assiduous prayer and penance."[10] In his commentary on Canon 603, Fr. Jean Beyer indicates that this paragraph of the canon "is very important for its doctrinal value."[11] Fr. Beyer explains: "The eremitic life is of itself solitary; it does not constitute an institute of consecrated life; it is and remains a venerable institution which is at the origin of monastic and religious life in the Church. Every Christian called by God to this kind of life can be made a hermit, on the condition that he is able to discern the divine will for his life and is aided by competent persons."[12] Discernment, as well as facilitation and oversight by competent persons, are addressed in the second paragraph of the canon. Canon 603.2 states that the juridical standing and recognition of the consecrated hermit requires the public profession of the three evangelical counsels of poverty, chastity, and obedience. In this regard, there is similarity to those in religious institutes. All consecrated hermits publicly profess the evangelical counsels, confirmed by vow or sacred bond, before their diocesan bishop. Doing so indicates a particular connection of the hermit to the local diocese in which she or he will reside, and to the diocesan bishop who will assume responsibility for oversight of the hermit. According to Canon 603.2, the diocesan bishop

---

hermits was in a set of preliminary canons, just before the section dealing with religious, societies, and secular institutes explicitly. The relocation of the canon further clarifies that these persons are not members of institutes. The rules of institutes provide adequately for members who seek greater solitude; reference to this has been removed from the universal law. The hermits spoken of in the canon relate directly to the diocesan bishop, making their public profession of the counsels in his hands. Such persons are recognized in law as living a consecrated life."

10. These features can be found in Canon 603.1. For a succinct explication of each of the elements of Canon 603, see MacDonald, "Hermits," 163–89.

11. Beyer, *Law of Consecrated Life*, 138.

12. Ibid.

oversees direction of the canonical hermit and of the hermit's obedience to the plan of life.[13]

The features identified in Canon 603 suggest that the canonical hermit has the ability to define certain key areas of his or her eremitic life and practice as a recognized form of consecrated life. The hermit's role in this process of self-definition creates a situation in which there is both a distinctiveness of practice, based on the decisions of the individual consecrated hermit, as well as diversity across practices that results from this distinctiveness. As in other forms of eremitic life and practice examined in earlier chapters, this process of self-definition occurs within an existing conceptual framework for the eremitic life, a framework in which there is a dialectical relationship between the form and function of the consecrated life of the canonical hermit. Called by the Holy Spirit to the consecrated life, the canonical hermit must discern the specific nature of his or her eremitic practice; such discernment is a spiritual, deeply personal matter. Moreover, such discernment will yield insight about how the specific call of the hermit will take form in the location and structure of the eremitic practice.

While the final decision is certainly contingent on the approval of the diocesan bishop, the location of the canonical hermit is determined independent of a pre-existing form, rule, or set of prescriptions. As a result, consecrated hermits can be found across the United States as the hermitage space is chosen by each individual hermit often in consultation with various parties including the diocesan bishop or an appointed representative, and/or the spiritual guide.[14] On the location of the hermitage site, Fr. Beyer writes that "to live a serious eremitic life, one must seek and demand this solitude of place and of life, where a real and profound silence is possible and can be maintained and deepened—far from urban habitations, on the shore of the sea, on an island, in the mountain, or in the forest."[15]

---

13. Canon 603.2. On this Beyer, *Law of Consecrated Life*, 141, writes: "Paragraph 2 of Canon 603 nowadays permits the public recognition of a hermit by the Church, and thus confers on him a state of life recognized by ecclesial law. Such a new fact in the Church became a necessary norm, given the growing number of hermits—men and women, laymen and priests." See also Hite et al., *Handbook on Canons*, 55: "The term 'religious' now applies to individuals with no obligation to common or community life and no relationship to an institute."

14. In addition to Beyer's 1988 commentary on Canon 603, see also Weisenbeck, *Vocation to Eremitic Life*, 104.

15. Beyer, *Law of Consecrated Life*, 139.

Location of practice is connected to the guidelines and structure under which the consecrated hermit will live. The rule, or plan of life, serves as the written guide for the daily life of the hermit and determines the structure of the eremitic life and practice. The consecrated hermit crafts the plan of life, again under the direction of the diocesan bishop or an appointed representative. The plan of life is approved by this authority as well.

A variety of resources for prospective hermits, as well as diocesan bishops, are currently available to assist with implementation and reflect the desire to balance the aims of the vocational call to eremitic life with canonical requirements and norms, in particular, those outlined in Canon 603.[16] Such resources provide guidance with criteria for discernment and qualifications, completion and filing of requisite forms, formation to the eremitical life, as well as matters pertaining to the hermit's lifestyle including policies and procedures about financial responsibility and personal property. Guidance is also available for the construction of the plan of life highlighting considerations for interpreting the elements defined in Canon 603 and the evangelical counsels of poverty, chastity and obedience. Resources for diocesan bishops stress spiritual matters including the need to facilitate discernment to the consecrated life of the hermit as well as oversight.

While the consecrated hermit may live entirely isolated from regular contact with others,[17] one form of expression available to the consecrated hermit who is called to live in closer proximity to other hermits in an isolated space may be the laura. The laura is an ancient structural form for eremitic life and practice in which a colony of hermits live in separate, solitary dwellings around a chapel or central house, and convene daily or weekly for liturgical prayer. In this form, hermits are under the direction of a spiritual director, who may live as well on the hermitage site, without being bound to the same rule or institute and without constituting a formal community. On this, Sister Marlene Weisenbeck, FSPA, author of *The Vocation to Eremitic Life*, writes that hermits agreeing to live in a group or

---

16. See the bibliography at the end of Weisenbeck, *Vocation to Eremitic Life*, for an excellent list of resources. Many works address specific aspects of the eremitic life. On this see, e.g., Russell, "Dangers of Solitude," 575–83, and Russell, "Must Hermits Work?," 159–74. Many dioceses now also include information about this form of consecrated life on their diocesan websites and publications. Many of the new responsibilities now included among the bishop's duties as a result of Canon 603 are discussed in MacDonald, "Hermits," 163–89.

17. The resources I reviewed advocated at least monthly contact between the hermit and his/her spiritual director and/or the diocesan bishop.

A Listening Presence

community "usually have their own personal living space (hermitage) and contribute in some way to the common financial expenses that provide for this way of life."[18]

The laura is the form used by the Hermits of Bethlehem, a mixed community of male and female hermits, guided by Abba Eugene Romano and overseen by the current diocesan bishop, Bishop Serratelli. In accordance with Canon 603, the Hermits of Bethlehem are neither a religious institute nor a coenobitic form of monasticism. As Abba Romano, the founder and Desert Father of the Hermits of Bethlehem, explains, "The hermits support one another in solitude while exercising a life of mature responsible freedom to adapt Bethlehem's way of living when necessary. The flexibility contrasts with monastic, community, cloistered living where most exercises are held in common."[19] Such flexibility does necessitate that there be some communal features of the eremitic life as it is defined by the Hermits of Bethlehem, however. The Hermits of Bethlehem support each other in their individual endeavors to live the eremitic life. They come together for celebration of the Eucharist and share in the exercise of charity and hospitality to others outside the hermitage site. Furthermore, each hermit contributes to the protection, economic stability and self-sufficiency of the hermitage site.[20]

In accordance with their juridical standing, the Hermits of Bethlehem serve the local diocesan community and the worldwide church as a "Bethlehem presence," in the spirit of the teachings of Scripture and the Desert Fathers by living a contemplative life,[21] cultivating wholeness of body, mind and spirit,[22] and exercising charity and hospitality.[23] In order to fulfill their vocation to serve as a "Bethlehem presence," the Hermits of Bethlehem dwell set apart from others. Their location, removed as it is from the busyness and business of daily life and yet simultaneously connected through these forms of service, creates an environment for contemplation, and is thus shaped by the intentions and activities that occur in the space of the hermitage site. In particular, the Hermits of Bethlehem seek to cultivate acts of listening as a spiritual practice in the silence of solitude. The cultiva-

18. Weisenbeck, *Vocation to Eremitic Life*, 22.
19. Romano, *Plan of Life of the Hermits of Bethlehem*, xx.
20. Ibid.
21. Ibid., 3.
22. Ibid., 39.
23. Ibid., 53.

tion of listening renders their location desert space and their presence in the context of their local diocese distinct. The listening cultivated by the Hermits of Bethlehem is founded upon common, shared eremitic practices of withdrawal (*anachoresis*) and ascetic discipline as defined by their plan of life found in *A Way of Desert Spirituality: The Plan of Life of the Hermits of Bethlehem*.

Because the listening presence of the Hermits of Bethlehem is a distinctive contribution to the study of eremitic practices in the United States, this chapter considers the construction, cultivation and impact of the Hermits of Bethlehem as a "Bethlehem presence" in the specific context of their local church. Our consideration will permit an examination of how listening functions as a defining characteristic of the specific eremitic vocation of these contemporary hermits.

The Plan of Life: A Guide for Eremitic Practice in Accordance with Canon 603

The story of the origins and early development of the Hermits of Bethlehem begins with its founder, Abba Eugene Romano. Abba Romano was ordained a diocesan priest in 1957, and he served in parish life until founding the Hermits of Bethlehem. As he explains to readers of the *Plan of Life*, his "persistent desire for the contemplative life"[24] compelled him to explore its forms over the years. In 1968, Abba Romano appealed to his local bishop, then Bishop Lawrence B. Casey, about the creation of a diocesan hermitage. Due to pastoral needs, it was not until 1973 that the bishop was able to affirm Abba Romano's request.[25]

A donation of land in Chester, New Jersey, located in Morris County and part of the Diocese of Paterson, became the site for the new hermitage. The hermitage name emerged from Abba Romano's experience of hearing the passage from St. Jerome's *Treatise on Psalm 95* that opens this chapter. Abba Romano heard these words while in prayer at a Holy Week retreat in 1975.[26] St. Jerome's words had an immediate impact on Abba Romano's resolve to establish an eremitical foundation, as he explains: "When I first heard these words, I felt they were a wonderful confirmation of my hope

---

24. Romano, *Plan of Life of the Hermits of Bethlehem*, 106.

25. Ibid., 107.

26. Ibid., 105. This draws attention to the religious significance of marking and naming space.

and my calling from God."²⁷ Gradually, from the mid-1970s to the present, the site has been converted with twelve hermitages, a common house, a chapel, and an access road. The site is intended to create and foster a Bethlehem presence, by bearing witness to the life and work of Jesus Christ through the eremitic practice.

Canonical recognition of the Hermits of Bethlehem has also occurred in stages. Preliminary endorsement of the *Plan of Life of the Hermits of Bethlehem* was given by then Bishop Frank J. Rodimer in 1987. After further revision and review of the *Plan of Life*, the Hermits of Bethlehem were then erected as a Public Association of the Christian Faithful by Bishop Rodimer in 1989. Final approval of the *Plan of Life* was given in 1992 by the bishop. In his letter to Abba Romano, the bishop draws attention to both the Christological foundation of the eremitic practice, as well as the significance of the *Plan of Life* for guiding this practice. The Hermits of Bethlehem received canonical status as a Laura of Consecrated Hermits of the Diocesan Right on December 8, 1997, the Feast of the Immaculate Conception. The Bethlehem Hermitage celebrated its thirtieth anniversary in 2005. For many, it was an opportunity to reflect the contributions of Abba Romano and the significance of the Hermitage site. Commemorating the occasion, one article that appeared in the diocesan newspaper, *The Beacon*, noted that "the hermitage's influence has extended well beyond the diocese's boundaries" through assistance to those in other dioceses seeking to establish hermitages.²⁸ The article concluded with Abba Romano's statement, "It's been a fruitful apostolate of prayer and spiritual guidance."²⁹

The principles governing the eremitic practice of the Hermits of Bethlehem are found in their *Plan of Life*. In this context, the term plan of life has a specific meaning, and it may help to adopt the practice of others by differentiating it from a monastic rule for the purposes of clarity. A plan of life is similar to a monastic rule in the sense that it provides a written framework for the cultivation of the particular form of religious practice, whether it be the eremitic or cenobitic form. However, despite this similarity, there is an important distinction between a plan of life and a monastic rule. Unlike a monastic rule, a plan of life corresponds not to those in religious institutes but rather to those who are consecrated hermits in accordance with Canon

---

27. Ibid.

28. See Wojcik, "Holy Ground" at http://www.patersondiocese.org/page.cfm?WebID=1424.

29. Ibid.

603.[30] That is, a plan of life corresponds to a form of practice specific to, and constructed in accordance with, the canonical status of its practitioners as consecrated hermits. In his commentary on Canon 603, Fr. Beyer emphasizes the significance of the plan of life for the consecrated hermit, writing that "the plan of life takes on major importance by the fact that it situates and governs his life and his various obligations."[31] It is important to note, as well, that the plan of life is a product of a call to eremitic practice and so emerges from the lived experience of the consecrated hermit.[32] While one plan of life may contain features in common with another plan of life, it is a personal document, in the sense that it is of primary use to the individual hermit whose life it organizes and governs. Abba Romano emphasizes this in the specific context of the Hermits of Bethlehem when he writes that the *Plan of Life* is not only a juridical document, "but more importantly, it is an attempt to unfold the charism of the desert in the framework of a lived experience," adding that it "is a spiritual reflection on our way of life."[33]

The *Plan of Life of the Hermits of Bethlehem* is a neatly organized document. Following an opening exhortation from Abba Romano, a prologue and an introductory statement that emphasizes the purpose of the eremitic life in general and of the practice of the Hermit of Bethlehem, in particular, the *Plan of Life* consists of six chapters and an epilogue. These chapters are intended to outline both the desert spirituality and practical guidelines of their eremitic life and practice. The *Plan of Life* treats the desert spirituality of the Hermits of Bethlehem first. Discussion of spiritual formation and eremitic life is contextualized closely by appeal to the example of the life of Jesus Christ, to the teachings of the gospels, to the historical lineage of the desert fathers and mothers, and to the conditions defined by Canon 603 in the *Revised Code of Canon Law*. Dwelling in desert space, in silence and in solitude, individual sections of chapters highlight the distinctive features of the eremitic life of those who adhere to the *Plan of Life*. The first three chapters of the *Plan of Life* focus specifically on the tripartite structure of the Bethlehem presence of the hermit and of the hermitage site. Although each element of this structure is presented individually, throughout is an

---

30. See Romano, *Plan of Life of the Hermits of Bethlehem*, prologue.

31. Beyer, *Law of Consecrated Life*, 143.

32. This is embedded consistently in the letters that reflect the developmental stages of the founding and consecration of the Hermits of Bethlehem that are included in Romano, *Plan of Life of the Hermits of Bethlehem*.

33. Romano, *Plan of Life of the Hermits of Bethlehem*, 105.

A Listening Presence

emphasis on unity in practice. The hermit's embodiment and life of a trinity of presence through love of God (ch. 1), of oneself (ch. 2), and of others (ch. 3) is the focus of eremitic life and practice. Given the central role of the trinity of presence to the eremitic life and practice of the Hermits of Bethlehem, these chapters will receive separate treatment in the following section.

The desert spirituality of the Hermits of Bethlehem, outlined as a trinity of presence in the first three chapters of the Plan of Life, emerges from the specific considerations defined for the consecrated hermit in Canon 603. Given this, chapter 4, "Introduction to the Vows: Living in the Mysteries of Christ; Imitating the Pattern of His Life," addresses directly the three evangelical counsels and their manifestation in the eremitic life and practice of the Hermits of Bethlehem. Here, the *Plan of Life* underscores, consistently, that humility is the basis for living poverty, chastity and obedience.[34]

There is a shift from discussion of desert spirituality to more practical guidelines and considerations in the remaining chapters of the *Plan of Life*. Chapter 5, "Formation: Transformation into Christ," outlines the stages of candidacy and of admission to the laura. These stages are: pre-entrance, provisional membership, and permanent membership. The daily *horarium*, as well as guidelines for the weekly Day of Reclusion, Sundays and Solemnities, are also included in this chapter. Chapter 6 focuses on matters pertaining more specifically to the administration of the hermitage site, including governance, finances and membership.

The epilogue closes the *Plan of Life* with reflections on the peace-filled, listening presence to be cultivated by the Hermits of Bethlehem. Prior discussion of desert spirituality and practical guidelines for eremitic life and practice culminate in a final statement about the place of the Hermits of Bethlehem in the Church and in the world. Returning to consider this, Abba Romano writes: "The Bethlehem Laura of Hermits is to be an oasis of peace. Guided by the light of Jesus it is to be open to His continual call, dedicating itself to live the eremitical life more deeply hidden in the Eucharistic Heart of Jesus so that before the Father and in the power of the Spirit the hermits may be transformed more and more into servants of His Gospel of peace and love."[35] Conscious and explicit appeal to the tri-partite structure of the eremitic practice of the Hermits of Bethlehem grounds this exhortation to serve as a place of peace. The deep need in the current age for peace, and for such a peace-filled presence is also emphasized and

---

34. Ibid., 59–62.
35. Ibid., 101.

further enhances the connection between the Hermits of Bethlehem and their ancient predecessors for whom this was also the case.

The core precept of the *Plan of Life of the Hermits of Bethlehem* is a single condition, as stated explicitly and from which emerges the entire structure of the practice of these hermits: "The essential condition is that the seeker consider the goal of life with God more important than anything else. For this goal, he is willing to sacrifice all the rest: to renounce all things, that he may follow Christ (cf. Matthew 19:21)."[36] The formation of a way of life in accordance with this condition and with the stipulations and guidelines of Canon 603 in the *Revised Code of Canon Law* places emphasis on the solitary nature of the eremitic vocation and on the solitude of the hermitage.[37] Solitary and in solitude, the life of the hermit entails a focus on the formation of the hermit's intellect through study, reading, spiritual direction, prayer and discernment under the direction of the Abba.[38] Not an end in itself, the interior formation of the individual hermit contains a significant exterior dimension as the *Plan of Life* explains: "In the eremitical life of solitude, the hermit continually strives to seek God above all for His own sake and to live every moment in His holy presence, growing in purity of heart in order to attain the perfection of charity."[39] Like the ancient desert fathers and mothers of the early church, whose teachings and example serve as a vital source of wisdom,[40] the Hermits of Bethlehem advocate a life that is centered in becoming a listening presence. Moreover, by adopting and adapting this ancient form of Christian life, the Hermits of Bethlehem hearken back to a historical lineage in Christian eremitic practice in a way that also responds to the needs of a current age.

Eremitic Practice: Defining and Cultivating a Listening Presence

The Hermits of Bethlehem, like several other forms of contemporary eremitic practice considered in this book, contextualize the physical presence

36. Ibid., 84.
37. Ibid., xvi–xvii.
38. Ibid., 47.
39. Ibid., xl.
40. Ibid., xxxvii: "Because the hermit life is rooted in the Gospel of Jesus Christ and lived in the tradition and spirit of the desert fathers of the early Church, each hermit pays special attention to their writings and teachings."

and form of their particular eremitic practice through the act of constructing and dwelling in desert space. Like their ancient counterparts, their desert space is set apart and removed from urban life. Again, like their predecessors, these hermits are not so isolated, however, so as to be inaccessible. Their withdrawal is for the purpose of leading a life of continuous prayer and worship. Indeed, it is precisely through their physical proximity and solidarity with others in the diocese in the context of their shared catholicity that the eremitic life and practice of the Hermits of Bethlehem creates a counter-cultural presence. The construction and operation of the listening presence of the Hermits of Bethlehem as a counter-cultural presence can be explored by examination of the *Plan of Life*.

Adherence to the *Plan of Life* creates an environment of desert wilderness that is identified in the *Plan of Life* in geographical and spiritual terms. In geographical terms, the desert wilderness of the Hermits of Bethlehem is defined by the physical space occupied by the eremitic settlement and its natural surroundings. Here, the desert is "a solitary place void of distracting elements, simple and uncluttered-a place of spiritual rest and spiritual combat-a place for listening to the word of God and heeding it."[41] The proper use of the geographic space for this purpose further characterizes the desert wilderness. Because the Hermits of Bethlehem envision their eremitic practice as a form emerging from the teachings and example of the desert fathers and mothers, they hearken directly to the spatial considerations of these early Christian hermits. The Hermits of Bethlehem do this, in part, by configuring their eremitic space in relation to the laura, an early Christian desert model for the eremitic practice in which a small number of hermits live in separate, solitary dwellings around several common buildings.[42] The decision of the Hermits of Bethlehem to map their eremitic space in these terms recalls in an intentional way both the solitude and silence of the eremitic call as well as its historical foundations in the early desert mothers and fathers.

The structure of the eremitic practice of the Hermits of Bethlehem also retains a key distinguishing feature prominent in the desert fathers and mothers in the form of the relationship between the hermit and his or her spiritual guide. As stipulated in the *Plan of Life*, each hermit is obedient to Father Romano, the Abba and Desert Father. In this capacity, Abba

---

41. Ibid., 116.

42. See the descriptions of the laura in Romano, *Plan of Life of the Hermits of Bethlehem*, xix.

Romano serves the Hermits of Bethlehem "by guiding each one in the way of desert spirituality and discerning with each one the best way to live his or her particular life within the laura according to Bethlehem's Plan of Life."[43] The Desert Father, Abba Romano, provides spiritual direction to each hermit by assisting with the task of discernment and by offering leadership through his example. In this way, Abba Romano serves the hermits through his imitation of the examples of Jesus and of the desert fathers. His oversight of the temporal needs of the laura includes the protection and safety of each hermit and assures shared labor for economic self-sustainment.[44]

The formation of a direct lineage between present and past practice through the spatial mapping of the hermitage site and the incorporation of the structural relationship between the abba and the individual hermit is further complemented by the Hermits of Bethlehem through consistent appeal to the lives and teachings of the ancient mothers and fathers of the desert. Here, too, such intentional appeal informs how the Hermits of Bethlehem define both the contours of interior formation and the element of exterior witness to the local and global community. Desert spirituality infuses the lives of the Hermits of Bethlehem. For this reason, like their ancient predecessors, the eremitic life of the Hermits of Bethlehem is rooted in the life of Jesus Christ and in gospel teachings; moreover, like their ancient predecessors, the *Plan of Life* of the Hermits of Bethlehem advocates a life of listening. The *Plan of Life* suggests that listening, as an eremitic activity, assumes both quantitative and qualitative features. Quantitatively, because the entire life of the hermit is given over to prayer, in contemplative silence and in solitude, it is a means of continuous listening to the Word of God. Formal times for prayer and contemplation, work, study, and all daily activities become opportunities for the hermit to be present to and aware of the divine will. Imbued with a heightened awareness, the cultivation of listening is qualitatively distinct.

In terms of spirituality, the desert wilderness in which the Hermits of Bethlehem dwell is defined by a state of being that may be realized in the space they have constructed; more specifically, it is defined by listening as a continuous awareness of the presence of the divine. As Abba Romano explains, the hermit "enters solitude with an intense yearning for Him and is led alone by God on a unique and private journey, responding to Him in secret. This is a hidden and private conversation of love with the Lord so

---

43. Ibid., xx.
44. Ibid., xxi.

that the word is made flesh in each hermit (cf. Jn 1:14)."[45] As a result, it is in the desert wilderness of the heart, the *Plan of Life* explains, that the Hermit of Bethlehem is led by the Holy Spirit of Jesus "purifying and transforming the hermit more and more into the image of God."[46] Such transformation is construed in explicit terms that, again, reflect both the interior formation and exterior witness of the Hermit of Bethlehem. In terms of interior formation, Jesus Christ is the model for the journey of obedience and surrender to the will of God undertaken by the individual hermit. The transformation of the individual hermit is, moreover, only possible because of Jesus Christ.[47] Interior formation yields exterior witness as the *Plan of Life* indicates: "The hermit enters into the silence and solitude of Jesus' Heart, there to still and quiet his own heart, there to learn what it is to be loved and cherished by God, there to experience the healing touch of love, there to hear the command, 'Love one another as I have loved you' (John 13:34). The love, healing and command of the Heart of Jesus empowers the hermit to extend the love of God to the entire human family by a hidden life of unceasing prayer and sacrifice."[48] And so, fed by prayer, "the bread of the hermit's life," the sacred scriptures, "the lungs of the hermit's daily prayer," and the Eucharistic sacrifice, "the heart of the hermit's day,"[49] the Hermit of Bethlehem seeks to become transformed and to cultivate a trinity of presence (listening): "a loving openness to God, to oneself, and to others."[50]

This trinity of presence may be represented as follows, wherein the simultaneous ordering of openness to God, to oneself, and to others in the heart of the hermit is represented separately here only as a means of considering the discrete elements that comprise the desert spirituality of the Hermits of Bethlehem.

---

45. Romano, *In the Silence of Solitude*, xix.
46. Romano, *Plan of Life of the Hermits of Bethlehem*, 17.
47. Ibid., xv-xvi, xix, xxiii.
48. Ibid., xxiii.
49. Romano, *In the Silence of Solitude*, xix.
50. Romano, *Plan of Life of the Hermits of Bethlehem*, 2.

Trinity of Presence and the Hermits of Bethlehem

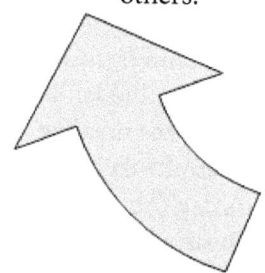
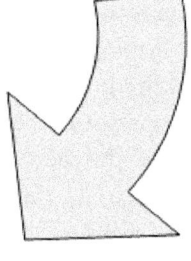

CHARITY AND HOSPITALITY
The hermit is a listening presence to God in others, thereby embodying a love of and for others.

CONTEMPLATIVE LIFE
The hermit is a listening presence to God as Creator and Father, thereby embodying a love of and for God.

INTEGRATED SELF
The hermit is a listening presence to God in oneself, thereby embodying a love of and for self.

According to their *Plan of Life*, the hermit is present to God as Creator and Father when the hermit freely[51] permits the self to be nourished by the divine presence encountered in the natural world of divine creation, in the silence and solitude of the hermitage, in the continuous prayer with and contemplation of the divine presence, and in solidarity with the Blessed Virgin Mary. Such nourishment is the foundation of the eremitic life and facilitates the embodiment of love of and for God. The hermit is present to the divine presence in the self, when the hermit freely cultivates an ascetic discipline of mind and body that enables the cultivation of love of and for

---

51. The term freely has a specific meaning in this context, as defined in Romano, *Plan of Life of the Hermits of Bethlehem*, 64, where freedom is an act of surrendering the self to the divine: "The hermit is not truly free unless he abandons himself to God's will."

the self. Finally, through charity in the laura and hospitality to visitors, the hermit is present to the divine presence in others. A deep recognition of solidarity with others through love, and in love, marks the charity and hospitality of the Hermits of Bethlehem.

As we have seen in our consideration of several other structures for the eremitic practice in previous chapters, the individual hermit may express the need for deeper solitude. The *Plan of Life* acknowledges that, over a lifetime, spiritual formation may lead the hermit to seek reclusion. Given this possibility, the cultivation of the eremitic life in accordance with *Plan of Life* recognizes that the hermit may be called to greater solitude than that provided by the weekly Day of Reclusion. For this reason, there is room for the possibility of a more temporary or permanent reclusion in the life of the hermit. If a deeper reclusion is requested and approved, the hermit "will be freed from all cares and responsibilities within the laura,"[52] and will receive material and spiritual necessities from the Desert Father who will continue oversight of, and receive obedience from, the hermit.

Eremitic Charity and Hospitality: Bearing Witness by Serving as a Listening Presence

In addition to the biblical texts, the Hermits of Bethlehem draw on a range of narrative sources for their practice. Close consideration is given to the writings of the Church Fathers, such as St. Jerome, in their eremitic practice. Likewise, the wisdom literature of the early desert fathers and mothers, including works such as the *Life of Antony* and the *Sayings of the Desert Fathers and Mothers*, are also incorporated. In order to get a sense of the ways in which such works are read and used, we may look more closely at the latter. The *Sayings of the Desert Fathers and Mothers*, a compilation of aphorisms and teachings reflecting desert eremitic life in late antique Egypt, highlights the dialogues, the conversations, that occurred between spiritual guides, their disciples, and unknown visitors from the nearby and surrounding areas. Looking for counsel, insight, and assistance, such visitors would arrive at the cell or dwelling of the identifiable guide unannounced and request a 'word.' Early efforts to create a record of the exchange between guide and visitor indicate belief in the relevance of such encounters and reflect a desire to preserve them for the purpose of oral and written transmission. The *Sayings* continue to serve as a source of spiritual

---

52. Ibid., 9.

guidance for many Christians, and especially for many Catholics, today. Certainly, the number of publications featuring the *Sayings* is evidence of sustained interest and application.[53]

In their capacity as a testimony to the centrality of the desert wilderness experience in the Christian life, the *Sayings of the Desert Fathers and Mothers* provide an important model for the desert spirituality of the Hermits of Bethlehem. Like their ancient predecessors, in the context of hospitality and charity, the listening presence of the Hermits of Bethlehem requires an intentional act of crossing boundaries into, and out of, the hermitage site. In particular, acts of hospitality and charity, of encounter and exchange, embedded in the desert spirituality of the *Sayings* is a feature of the eremitic life of the Hermits of Bethlehem. As with other forms of adoption and adaptation of ancient desert spirituality, these acts assume a distinctive quality for the Hermits of Bethlehem.[54] In accordance with the *Plan of Life*, and the practice of the ancient desert fathers and mothers, the Hermits of Bethlehem "receive Christ in every guest."[55] As a result, desert hospitality is defined as a "welcoming and silent presence"[56] whereby a guest is provided with a hermitage for a week or a weekend. The guidelines for the "Hermitage Experience" in the *Plan of Life* explain that "by the living witness of the hermit's life of prayerful silence and solitude, the guest is gently led into the desert of his/her own heart, to grow in live and adoration of the Triune God."[57] This atmosphere of prayer offers an opportunity for healing and renewal in the solitude and silence of the Hermitage. Like their ancient predecessors, hospitality is a means of bearing witness as the Hermits of Bethlehem "hope to share with others, through desert hospitality, the depth and beauty of communion with God."[58] Spiritual direction as well as the sacraments of penance and Eucharist, are also made available to those who visit the site as guests.

---

53. This is reflected as well in the variety of approaches to examination of the Sayings. One might contrast, for example, the approach taken by Keller, *Oasis of Wisdom*, with that taken by Gruen, *Heaven Begins with You*.

54. See Romano, *Plan of Life of the Hermits of Bethlehem*, xxi, especially the third item on the list for hermits: "The exercise of loving charity and desert hospitality (the ancient hermits were about what any Christian at any time in history must be about, the love of God and neighbor)."

55. Ibid., 55.

56. Ibid.

57. Ibid., 56.

58. Romano, *In the Silence of Solitude*, xxxviii.

A Listening Presence

The observations and responses of such visitors to the Hermits of Bethlehem supply an important interpretation of the practical and ideological implications of their efforts to exercise hospitality and charity. Exercised with discretion, in order to "safeguard the eremitical life of silence, solitude and prayer,"[59] the Bethlehem Hermits receive priests, religious and laity to experience the silence of solitude. Testimonies of visitors to the Hermits of Bethlehem, available in the collection, *In the Silence of Solitude: Contemporary Witnesses of the Desert* (1995), describe the experience of hospitality as a "warm spirit of welcome"[60] and repeatedly as an opportunity for healing and renewal[61] in an environment where the hermits are said to "overflow with joy and kindness as they serve silently the needs of retreatants and each other."[62] Many visitors, like this one, emphasize the effects of the hospitality of the hermits: "There is a yearning for more of the same and an inclination to make one's own environment as much like Bethlehem as it can be."[63] In their definition of practice, and of the heart as the site of the real desert wilderness experience, the Hermits of Bethlehem are participating in the ongoing development of a desert hermeneutic contextualized by an encounter with the desert fathers. Despite a different social location, the Hermits of Bethlehem seek an effect that is similar to the effect acquired by their ancient counterparts. This effect is seen in the experience of visitors for whom the Hermits of Bethlehem serve as a holy presence and model for encountering God in contemporary society. As one visitor observed, "These hermits portray the power of God, not as the world depicts power but in the strength of silent, gentle, loving lives lived in service to those who come to seek the Lord. Their service stretches out in a loving, sacrificial, mysterious way to those who live amidst the turmoil of the world."[64] This observance emphasizes the potential value of the hermitage site as a constructed space, symbolizing for some the potency of the eremitic practice of the Hermits of Bethlehem. Moreover, this observation reinforces the idea that through the exercise of charity and hospitality, the hermitage site of the Hermits of Bethlehem is further transformed into a listening presence. Through the cultivation of listening, as a multi-faceted,

59. Romano, *Plan of Life of the Hermits of Bethlehem*, 56.
60. Romano, *In the Silence of Solitude*, 88.
61. Ibid., 89.
62. Ibid., 88.
63. Ibid.
64. Ibid., 95.

religious practice, on the part of the hermits and visitors, the hermitage site becomes a distinct space with a specific purpose.

The Hermits of Bethlehem appear to maintain a welcome and steady presence in their local diocese, the Diocese of Paterson, New Jersey. Their presence has been recognized along with other forms of consecrated life in the diocese. Diocesan commemoration of those living the consecrated life occurs through the celebration of World Day for Consecrated Life. The consecrated life has also been the subject of the bishop's weekly column which appears in *The Beacon*, the newspaper of the diocese. In one of his weekly columns, titled "Consecrated Life: Icon of the Church, Icon of God," Bishop Serratelli appeals directly to the role of those professing the consecrated life to the life of the diocese. Likening the consecrated life to a visible icon that points to an invisible reality, the bishop highlights one of the specific features that distinguish the consecrated life, namely the cultivation of the three evangelical counsels of poverty, chastity, and obedience. The bishop writes: "Living the evangelical counsels supports a spirituality of true communion where we think of our brothers and sisters in faith within the profound unity of the Mystical Body. It is no longer my life, but Christ who lives in me and shares with me the gift of divine life. To live the counsels effectively, to achieve such spirituality, requires a heart that constantly contemplates and stands in wonder of the Trinity dwelling within us."[65] While their status is recognized in these terms in the context of their specifically religious worldview, the Hermits of Bethlehem acknowledge that it can appear otherwise in the context of American society where the eremitic life is defined, at times, as counter-cultural in negative terms. The Hermits of Bethlehem, like their ancient counterparts, embrace both identifications. Affirming the universal and particular role of the hermit and of the eremitic life, Abba Romano explains that the hermit is "a martyr of conscience who gives witness to God's existence, supremacy and absoluteness, in a hedonistic and pleasure-seeking world which Pope John Paul II describes as a culture of death."[66] By striving to live as a listening presence "in the midst of a troubled world,"[67] the Hermits of Bethlehem are bearing witness to an ancient way of holiness in a radically different

---

65. See Bishop Serratelli's remarks in "Consecrated Life," in the diocesan publication *The Beacon*; archives available at http://www.patersondiocese.org.

66. See Romano, *Plan of Life of the Hermits of Bethlehem*, xix and viv. Here, Abba Romano draws attention to Pope John Paul II, *Gospel of Life* [Evangelium Vitae], #12.

67. Ibid., 109.

contemporary context. By participating in the ongoing development of a desert hermeneutic in their local diocese, by constructing a way of being that is contextualized by an encounter with the divine in the "desert wilderness," the Hermits of Bethlehem are issuing a recognizable and familiar response to this "world." Thus, what their acts of charity and exercise of hospitality indicate, what their reception by other consecrated persons and their diocesan bishop suggest, is that within their local diocese the eremitic life and listening presence of the Hermits of Bethlehem is a model for a way of hearing and of being the Word of God.

The Hermits of Bethlehem are evidence of an ancient way of life and, more particularly, of an ancient eremitic practice that is rooted in Christian desert spirituality. By embracing the call "to live at the heart of the Church, to reflect the mind of the Church,"[68] as hermits in accordance with the stipulations of Canon 603, the Hermits of Bethlehem promote a Christian life dedicated wholly and completely to praise of God and salvation of the world in stricter separation and solitude. By adhering to their *Plan of Life*, their lives are grounded in becoming a listening presence, in bearing witness and in charity.

A Shared Commitment

The canonical or consecrated hermit received juridical status in the *Revised Code of Canon Law* nearly twenty years ago. Canon 603, which outlines the guidelines for this status, marks a significant moment in the history of eremitic life and practice in the Roman Catholic Church. Through foundational ties to the diocese and diocesan bishop, canonical or consecrated hermits are connected in a specific way to their local church communities. Although removed from others in their life and practice, in a sense canonical or consecrated hermits are also connected to one another through their shared commitment to the evangelical counsels and vocation to the eremitic life. Across the United States, the impact of the canonical or consecrated hermit continues to grow and to be adopted in a variety of forms.

Canon 603 is the framework for a unique relationship between the canonical or consecrated hermit and the diocesan bishop. Episcopal involvement in the eremitic life and practice occurs on nearly every level. The individual works directly with the diocesan bishop throughout the discernment process. The bishop facilitates with theoretical, practical, and

---

68. Ibid., xv.

spiritual matters pertaining the implementation of Canon 603 and the hermit's life and practice. For example, from the individual's decision to accept the vocation to eremitic life and practice to the completion of administrative tasks and required forms that must be in place for consecration, the bishop assumes an important responsibility for the hermit as a member of his diocesan community. His oversight of the hermit's life and practice eremitic life and practice is an essential element in the entire process of spiritual formation.

Canon 603 is also the framework for a unique relationship between the canonical or consecrated hermit and the members of the local church community. The canonical or consecrated hermit is a member of the local church who bears witness through the eremitic vocation. Moreover, mutual support and solidarity between the hermit and the local church community are expressed through prayer and the central ritual of the Mass.

Canonical or consecrated hermits can be found in dioceses across the United States. Canonical or consecrated hermits represent a rich diversity in the specific location and particular expression of their practice. Whereas some hermits dwell near others in a configuration resembling a laura, an ancient structure used by a group of hermits living in proximity and gathering occasionally, other hermits choose to live alone in a single dwelling. Canonical or consecrated hermits are affiliated with dioceses of varying populations and sizes. Some are connected to dioceses in areas heavily populated by Roman Catholics; others reside in dioceses with fewer churches separated by greater distance.

The Hermits of Bethlehem offer one form that hearkens to a life in the desert as a contemplative, listening presence. Through the exercise of hospitality and charity, they extend this presence to others. Like the Hermits of Bethlehem, other forms employ their respective plans to guide their individual eremitic vocation and to realize their calling.

6

Framing a Worldview in Solitude

> Hermits observe no uniform rule of life. While some live in isolation, others are united in loosely organized communities which have sometimes formed the nucleus of a new monastery or order.[1]

A SEEMINGLY RANDOM REQUEST FOR EXAMPLES OF CHRISTIAN HERMITS can conjure images of ancient desert ascetics or medieval anchoresses dwelling in cells attached to churches; the same appeal in the context of a secular worldview could prompt reflection on the transcendentalists or the isolated shack in the remote mountains of Alaska. The shared focal point in all of these examples is that, regardless of specific context, we tend to envisage and identify the hermit by his or her otherness, a category that recognizes the hermit as an individual who has chosen to adopt an atypical life marked by a degree of withdrawal and separation from the norms of the dominant society. To a certain extent, there is an element of accuracy in this initial depiction. Hermits are social outliers in the sense that, although they are connected to the dominant society, the hermit's degree of physical and emotional distance from the daily life of that society characterizes them as simultaneously distinct and different from other more mainstream members of the population.

As we have seen in previous chapters, this degree of eremitic withdrawal and separation is defined and interpreted in the context of the specific form of eremitic life embraced by the hermit. That is, each of the eremitic forms considered in previous chapters illustrates a particular understanding of the relationships between the individual hermit, the immediate eremitic community, and the dominant society; furthermore, these

---

1. See "Hermit," *Oxford Dictionary of the Christian Church*, 766.

relationships are framed by an operative understanding that corresponds to the specific mission of the religious order, institute, or vocation to which the hermit is called.

Social Relationships and Eremitic Life and Practice

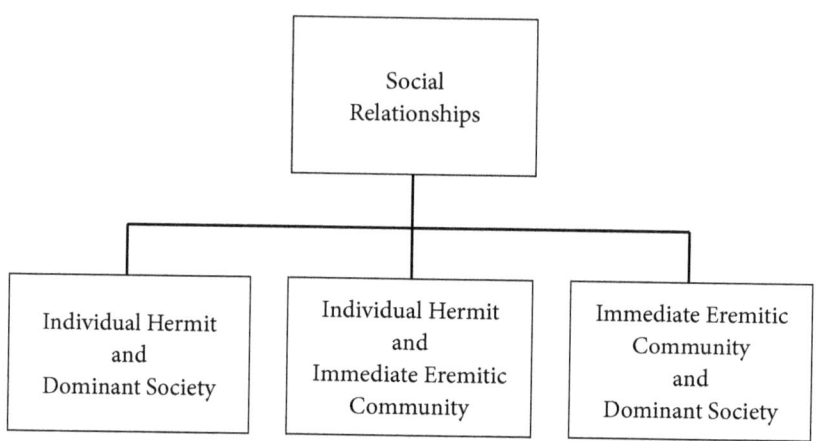

Acknowledgement of these formative narratives and contexts grounds these relationships in a longstanding tradition and history that recognizes why and how the relationships between the individual hermit and the dominant society, between the individual hermit and his or her own immediate eremitic community, and between the immediate eremitic community and the dominant society are all foundational to the eremitic life and practice. We have seen, as well, that eremitic reclusion is no exception here, as these relationships are found even within the individual structures for reclusion. Among those eremitic forms that include the possibility for reclusion, the hermit's withdrawal and separation from the dominant society, and within the immediate eremitic community, are constructive and connected. The recluse, like the other hermits in affiliation, remains bounded by the specific context of the form of eremitic life and practice that has been professed in accordance with the respective constitutions, statutes, and plans of life. According to each of the eremitic forms reviewed in previous chapters, reclusion is granted only by permission and remains connected to the community through regular formal oversight by the abbot or spiritual father, by the vow of obedience and by the cultivation of charity. Although reclusion entails that the hermit undertakes an additional form of withdrawal from the other

Framing a Worldview in Solitude

members of his or her community for the purpose of a more solitary form of practice, reclusion is understood consistently and explicitly as a further means of contributing to the life and welfare of the immediate community of hermits. Because reclusion is an extension of an existing, established form of practice, its purpose and place within the specific eremitic forms in which it is found is clearly situated and defined.

The qualitative and quantitative distinctiveness of eremitic withdrawal and separation appears acutely in the construction of solitude. For, regardless of the specific eremitic form, the hermit's withdrawal and separation from societal life entail the espousal of solitude as a primary value that is prioritized and privileged.[2] Put simply, solitude is a fundamental feature of the eremitic life present in all of its many and varied forms. With regard to the specific forms of eremitic life and practice presented in previous chapters, we have seen that solitude operates as a value defined not only by the individual hermit but also by the immediate eremitic community; furthermore, the value and definition of solitude are always framed and interpreted in the context of a Roman Catholic worldview. This chapter seeks to move from close consideration of select evidence for the cultivation of solitude in the particular contexts of the eremitic forms as presented in previous chapters to explore several theoretical considerations for thinking more broadly about the place and function of eremitic solitude as a component of a Roman Catholic contemplative life. As we saw in the various interpretations of withdrawal and separation from societal life that characterize as distinct the many forms of eremitic solitude, the solitude of the hermit is also situated in the context of the eremitic community as defined by, and in accordance with, the applicable prevailing constitutions, statutes, and plans of life. For this reason, throughout discussion, we will need to keep in mind that eremitic solitude is simultaneously a feature of the life of the immediate eremitic community.

The singular focus on eremitic solitude in this chapter is not intended at the expense of the other features of eremitic life and practice; rather, such focus on solitude is intended as an exploration of one of the foundational

---

2. See Skudlarek, *Demythologizing Celibacy*, 1, who maintains that solitude as a value extends to cenobitic monastic forms "because a monastic community is not simply a gathering of like-minded individuals who enjoy one another's company and work together on a common project. It is, rather, an intentional community whose members are dedicated to the work of spiritual growth and who together fashion an environment in which each can engage in that inner work with a minimum of distractions." See also Stewart, *Prayer and Community*, 71–87.

organizing features of eremitic life and practice. Furthermore, the treatment of solitude in this chapter is neither comprehensive nor complete; as such, the chapter outlines several theoretical considerations by which we might then imagine some of the ways in which solitude operates as a religious category, as a lived experience partially witnessed by others in the forms of eremitic life and practice included in previous chapters. By taking the experience of solitude as our starting point, and by appealing to those basic dimensions that help to shape a religious worldview it may be possible to illumine further both the distinctive features of solitude in the particular contexts studied in previous chapters, as well as some of the ways in which the actions of, and language about, eremitic life and practice frames a distinctively contemplative interpretation of solitude in the broader context of Roman Catholicism.[3] Doing so heightens the connectedness to others that remains a component of these forms of eremitic solitude.

Defining Eremitic Solitude

How can the topic of eremitic solitude be approached by a non-practitioner? We might first ask this question about eremitic solitude in a general way, thereby posing a query that would address the nature of solitude as a human predicament or, in developmental terms, of the human need for temporary periods of withdrawal as an important opportunity for personal formation or self-reflection. Should we wish to pursue a different, though related, direction of inquiry we might ask this opening question more specifically about a particular form, or forms, of eremitic solitude. Our query might then be focused on either the distinct practice of solitude or on a cluster of practices that foster and shape eremitic life. At some point our question may prompt discussion of those contexts in which eremitic solitude is located, that is, of those social, political and environmental factors, among many others, in which solitude is lived and practiced. Our opening question will then require revision in order to give attention to the specific

---

3. Given the extensive body of scholarship on the topic of worldviews, for the purpose of discussion here, a specific meaning will be employed. By worldview in this context, I propose the application of those dimensions outlined in Smart, *Worldviews*. Again, this application is intended as a heuristic one. Smart delineates six dimensions of a worldview: experience, myth, doctrine, ritual, ethics, and social. McBrien, *Catholicism*, chs. 2 and 5 marks a similar typology for explaining Catholicism by highlighting faith (which shares elements of Smart's experience) which produces several outcomes of faith such as theology, doctrine, worship and morality.

detail of the form or forms of eremitic solitude under consideration. If it is the case that eremitic solitude is to be contextualized by a religious worldview, then the initial question could be recast to ask how eremitic solitude might be interpreted as a religious value or, more directly, the extent to which the experience of solitude is a requirement for understanding or for explaining solitude as a religious value. This returns us to the issue of access, namely, in what terms might a non-practitioner explore how eremitic solitude is interpreted through, and functions in, the context of a religious worldview?

At first glance, it may appear nonsensical or even impossible to propose a theoretical framework for the study of eremitic solitude in the context of a religious worldview and more specifically in the context of a Roman Catholic worldview. In this context, eremitic solitude occurs in and through the contemplative life which is, by definition, both deeply spiritual and highly personal. Certainly one could argue that, given the highly individualized nature of eremitic solitude and the distinctiveness of its expression in a multiplicity of forms in a Christian worldview, there is an element of inaccessibility that would prohibit attempts to accurately understand and explain eremitic solitude. And yet, there have been, and currently are, many studies of eremitic solitude written by both practitioners and non-practitioners alike which indicate that an examination and consideration of solitude are worthwhile and beneficial endeavors. In addition, if one starts with the premise that solitude is a basic human encounter of existential importance, then there is a common experience on which accessibility rests. As we will see, this common experience may have relevant implications for an approach to the study of eremitic solitude. Perhaps, then, rather than defying explanation, it is possible for a non-practitioner to gain some understanding of this multi-dimensional, multi-faceted human phenomenon.

How has eremitic solitude been approached as a topic of study? There are some studies of eremitic solitude that confront the apparent limitations and restrictions on understanding and explanation directly by indicating that the specificity of forms of eremitic life actually reveals a telling and useful plurality of perspective; as a result, descriptive accounts, practitioner insights, and non-practitioner encounters are garnered and presented as valuable evidence for some of the ways solitude is defined and lived as a primary personal value. While this approach readily acknowledges that, for example, some practitioner perspectives on solitude may be narrow in scope or in terms of accessibility, this approach is based on what is recounted and known in and through individual and communal experience; for this reason, practitioner views of, and reflections on, the experience of eremitic solitude provide evidence for how eremitic solitude is defined and functions as a value on personal, communal and universal levels.

There is much to be gained from exploration of the wide body of literature and scholarship on eremitic solitude. Sources authored by practitioners are typically rich in description and reflection, therein supplying important observations not only about reasons for, but also about a life of, withdrawal and anonymity; sources by non-practitioners range from surveys of types and forms of practice to close analysis of specific individuals or writings about solitude. Likewise, there are sources directed more specifically to those who may have an interest in pursuing eremitic solitude and others with a different audience in mind. Whereas some sources are autobiographical in nature, describing lessons lived and learned through a life of solitude, other sources betray different motives for authorship. While it is not possible to provide a thorough or comprehensive review and examination of sources here, it will be useful to consider select insights from a few recent sources that illumine both the considerable diversity in the approaches taken to the study of solitude as well as some of the contemporary questions being addressed about solitude. Even a brief presentation and discussion of some of these insights can inform a theoretical perspective on eremitic solitude. To this end, we will look briefly here at a few of the studies on the topic of solitude published over the period of a decade covering 1994–2004.[4] These studies uphold solitude as a value; however, as we will see, each study contributes to how solitude is defined as a value thereby exposing the multi-faceted, dynamic expression of solitude in this way. Furthermore, the authors of these studies give close attention to their

---

4. Here, too, the literature is broad and deep and there are many fine sources of study. Included among the studies on eremitic solitude are two sources composed by members of the Order of St. Benedict. One source is Hall, *Silence, Solitude, Simplicity*. The title of this work is illustrative in light of the forms of eremitic life and practice considered in previous chapters. In her work, Hall shares frank observations and theological reflection from the over twenty years she spent living as a hermit. She draws attention to the distinctive orientation of the eremitic life; the title of her work reflects both what the eremitic life and practice espouses as well as the particular way of seeing and of being in relation to others and to the world that grounds eremitic life and practice. The *Rule of Benedict* claims that experienced monks can pass from the cenobitic to the eremitic state (*RB* 1). Benedict, himself, spent a considerable amount of time living as a hermit. Another useful source by a Benedictine author and hermit is Bunge, *Earthen Vessels*. For a different approach and perspective on solitude, see Storr, *Solitude*.

respective motives for authorship and to their approach to the study of solitude. In each of these studies, it is noteworthy that an explicit recognition of the motivation for authorship contributes to the framing of the questions asked about solitude and factors into decisions about the scope and nature of the approach taken to the study of solitude.[5] Together, these studies allow us to consider a variety of angles and perspectives on solitude. By looking at these studies together and in the order of publication here, albeit briefly, we come to realize that while there are many possible approaches to the study of eremitic solitude, a cross-examination of select insights from these studies draws attention to the ways in which eremitic solitude has been defined and lived and, furthermore, to some of the ways in which solitude is functioning as a human, personal, religious value with several fundamental factors that appear across the variety of forms of eremitic life and practice. Collectively, then, these studies raise significant questions about whether, and how, solitude contributes to individual and collective identity and, thus, they contribute to an understanding of how solitude operates in a given worldview.

In his work *Solitude: A Philosophical Encounter*, published in 1994, Philip Koch raises fundamental questions about defining and evaluating solitude. Opening the first chapter of the book, "Dimensions," by framing an approach to the topic that presents, explores, discusses, and explains examples of solitude across historical and cultural contexts and time periods, Koch provides an operative definition of solitude that forms the foundation for subsequent unpacking, refining, discussion, and scrutiny in the remainder of his work. In this first chapter Koch asks, "What, then, is solitude? It is a time in which experience is disengaged from other people. All of the other features of solitude that come intuitively to mind, the physical isolation, the reflective cast of mind, the freedom, the silence, the distinctive feel of space and time-all of these flow from that core feature, the absence

---

5. There are many fine studies of eremitic solitude. Among these are included, for example, Halpern, *Migrations to Solitude*; Koch, *Solitude*; Colegate, *Pelican in the Wilderness*; Barbour, *Value of Solitude*. For a study that examines solitude in the context of the desert fathers, see Gould, *Desert Fathers on Monastic Community*, 139–66. Of solitude in the context of the withdrawal of early Christians to farms or to monastic or eremitic life and practice, it will be useful to include the following observation made by Sayre, *Solitude in Society*, 196: "In literature these solitudes are associated with mythical images of ideal community; and the retreats themselves-estate or monastery-are pictured as more harmonious communities than the society which is left behind. Even the isolated hermit, or the landowner alone in his study, communes with God, Nature, and other men."

of others in one's experiential world."⁶ The heightened emphasis on the element of disengagement, "the absence of others in one's experiential world," not only provides a structural basis for the study of solitude but also qualifies solitude in personal and social terms.⁷ Koch's insight supplies language for a discussion of solitude and raises awareness of the need to avoid dismissive or oversimplified definitions, especially through his consideration of the type of disengagement that grounds solitude. The operational definition provided emphasizes that distinctive element of solitude that facilitates application and evaluation broadly and in a wide range of contexts.

The ability of this definition, and of the type of disengagement that solitude maintains, to be tested in this way proves important in the final chapter of the book, a chapter titled "A Universal Value?" The chapter contains a deeply engaging discussion of whether solitude can be considered a universal value. Considerations of the meaning of the individual in ancient and medieval times, and in a range of cultural and religious contexts prompts the observation towards the end of the chapter that, "Inescapably situated in social and intimate nexes, yet touched by some dim sense of the nourishing and fulfilling power of solitary spiritual transcendence- this is the common human plight. The human Way, accordingly, leads not towards denial of either human relationship or inner transcendence, but along a road which winds through both territories."⁸

The identification of a relationship between solitude and connectedness to others is raised and advanced as well in the context of a particular worldview by author Isabel Colegate in her study of eremitic solitude, *A Pelican in the Wilderness: Hermits, Solitaries and Recluses*, published in 2002. With regard to current religious, or "holy," hermits, Colegate writes that "the extent to which the solitary religious life is lived today is probably known only to the hermits' respective sustaining networks; by the nature of their calling they are unobtrusive."⁹ These words signal a reminder that the eremitic life and practice promotes an element of intended elusiveness. Colegate's observation can serve further as a significant caution against generalizations about the lived experience of solitude as well as a reminder that the eremitic life is most often hidden from public view and may therefore foster anonymity. In practical terms, when applied to our examination

---

6. Koch, *Solitude*, 27.
7. Ibid., 57–79.
8. Ibid., 296.
9. Colegate, *Pelican in the Wilderness*, xiii.

Framing a Worldview in Solitude

of select forms of eremitic life and practice in previous chapters, Colegate's observation underscores the fundamental fact that on a very basic level the hermit often intends a lack of public visibility; although the forms of eremitic life and practice presented in previous chapters are known, in the sense that there is published, available information about them, there is an element of the unknown shaped by these forms of eremitic withdrawal and solitude whose conditions remain preserved and intact.

We might apply Colegate's observation as well to another important element of eremitic solitude, namely, the presence of a "sustaining network" in the life of the hermit. Herein is the allusion to some form of community, to some connection with others that serves as a structure of support for the hermit. As we have seen in the practices presented in previous chapters, the support offered and provided to the hermit by the "sustaining network," in this case, of fellow practitioners who share obedience and unity in the respective rules, constitutions, declarations, or plan of life of the specific eremitic form, may range widely and include, for example, material contributions as well as immaterial ones such as fellowship and solidarity with the hermit through prayer.

Such support, as a feature of the relationship between the community and eremitic solitude, is brought out as well by John D. Barbour in his slightly more recent study published in 2004, *The Value of Solitude: The Ethics and Spirituality of Aloneness in Autobiography*.[10] With regard to our discussion of eremitic solitude, Barbour's work includes study of solitude in the context of a Christian worldview. In an early chapter titled "Christian Solitude," Barbour considers evidence in the Christian tradition for eremitic solitude and, after exploration, observes: "The spiritual meaning of Christian solitude is not simply a matter of the motivations of hermits but also involves how these individuals were supported by a cultural context and a web of social relationships. Solitaries depend on other people both for the physical necessities of existence and for recognition and confirmation of their social role as solitaries. Hermits are strengthened to persist when they believe they provide something valued by their contemporaries."[11] This insight locates a relationship, or dialectic of sorts, between the hermit and those others with whom the hermit is connected. This relationship is built not only on the need for material support, but also on the need for

---

10. Barbour, *Value of Solitude*, 215, acknowledges the influence of Koch's study on his thinking about solitude.

11. Ibid., 27.

public validation of their status as hermits. When we apply Barbour's keen observation about the mutuality between the hermit and his or her "social relationships" to the evidence of eremitic life and practice examined in previous chapters, we can see the significance of context as a means of outlining the "recognition and confirmation" of status. In the evidence of select forms of eremitic life and practice in previous chapters, it is the constitutions, rules, and plans of life of the hermit and the eremitic community that contain statements and teachings about eremitic solitude that serve to contextualize this evidence. As a result of contextualization, the observer of eremitic life can be moved to position a practitioner's descriptive account of eremitic solitude from the particular, personal level into a larger narrative interpretive framework. This broader contextualization could then serve to open the possibility for explanation and understanding on a larger and more inclusive level. Furthermore, direct attention to key ecclesiastical teachings about contemplative life and eremitic practice would contribute an additional, necessary means of contextualizing both the individual experience, and the place in the immediate eremitic community, of eremitic solitude.

Framing Eremitic Solitude

Having briefly considered a few of the basic definitional and relational elements of eremitic solitude, we may now turn to the task of imagining a theoretical framework for eremitic solitude in the context of the Roman Catholic Church. How, then, do the elements of withdrawal and relationship work together in eremitic solitude in this context? More specifically, how is the hermit both removed from and simultaneously connected to others as a Roman Catholic hermit dwelling in the United States? We might begin to propose a response to these questions by appeal to the article "Eremitism: Call to the Chronically Ill and Disabled," in which author Sr. Laurel M. O' Neal offers a provocative insight about solitude. Her observations, while not specifically addressing the forms we have discussed in previous chapters, can help to frame our thinking about eremitic solitude in these contexts. O'Neal writes: "Solitude is, after all, the most catholic of all vocations, and a specifically eremitic vocation to solitude serves to remind us of its basic importance in the life of every person, not only as existential predicament, but as Christian value, challenge, and call."[12] O'Neal's insight indicates one

12. O'Neal, "Eremitism," 235.

way by which we might explore eremitic solitude in the specific contexts of the forms examined in previous chapters; in particular, her words indicate that there are at least three angles from which we might consider how solitude operates in the life of the hermit. If we apply each of these three angles to the particular contexts of eremitic life and practice treated in previous chapters, we will be able to explore not only those features specific to a particular angle of solitude but also the common, shared features of eremitic solitude. Thus, we might ask, what does it mean to consider solitude, as it is embodied in the forms of eremitic life and practice considered in previous chapters, from this perspective?

A response begins with recognition of solitude as a universal "existential predicament." The individual encounter with one's contingency is, at its core, a solitary one. In a very real and necessary sense, each human individual encounters questions of meaning and purpose. In this way, solitude is the fundamental state of being central to the life of each individual human person. The existential thrust of the human person into the world and the confrontation of one's contingency, require answers. Often, these answers are situated in the context of a worldview. Solitude, as the experience at the center of one's worldview, not only recognizes the need to confront the "existential predicament" at the heart of human experience but to do so in a way that offers a range of responses in the context of that worldview.

The Christian worldview offers a response to this existential predicament that accepts solitude as a "value, challenge, and call" by framing the predicament in an unfolding context of salvation history. In a Christian worldview, the response to questions of contingency, of meaning and purpose, are located in the life of Jesus Christ and in the teachings of the sacred scriptures. These sources locate and provide evidence for solitude as "Christian value, challenge, and call." The Roman Catholic worldview contributes significantly to the way that solitude is identified as "Christian value, challenge, and call." The specific "eremitic vocation to solitude" is, as a more specific form of life and practice in the Roman Catholic worldview, a means of embodying a call to follow the example of Jesus Christ in the divine presence. The specific forms of eremitic life and practice presented in previous chapters have drawn attention to some of the common, general features of the "eremitic vocation to solitude" in the Roman Catholic context including withdrawal, silence, prayer, and penance.[13]

13. See also Hart, *Thomas Merton*, 124: "Solitude has its own special work: a deepening of awareness that the world needs. A struggle against alienation. True solitude is deeply aware of the world's needs."

Seeking in Solitude

We might visualize the intersection of these three aspects of solitude (solitude as existential encounter; solitude as a component of the Christian worldview; solitude as a distinctively Roman Catholic value) as three concentric circles, each circle linking with the other two circles so that they overlap slightly with one another and converge at a central point. If we imagine for a moment that the Roman Catholic hermit is the point of intersection, we might envision how the individual encounter with solitude obtained in the eremitic life is necessarily and distinctly informed by all three aspects of solitude simultaneously. By envisioning the eremitic life in these terms, we may be able to acknowledge, at least on the surface, the distinctiveness of the eremitic life.

Aspects of Solitude in Eremitic Life and Practice

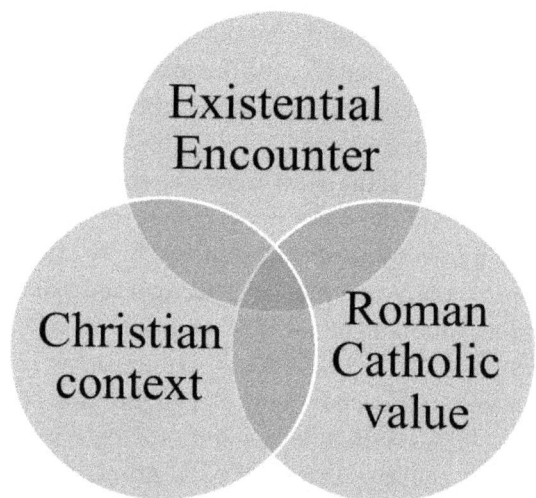

If we attempt to situate the Roman Catholic hermit in this way, then, we begin with the fact that it is in the particular context of the Roman Catholic worldview that the hermit locates a response to questions of meaning and value; in this way the eremitic life is a means of confronting one's contingency and finding meaning in and for one's life and purpose. Specifically, the eremitic vocation of solitude for the Roman Catholic hermit is a means of dwelling in the divine presence in a life of solitary contemplation that is defined in accordance with church teaching, and doctrine and tradition. The plurality of forms examined in previous chapters of this book,

Framing a Worldview in Solitude

therefore, highlights some of the many ways the eremitic life is interpreted in, and shaped by, this particular context. Furthermore, as we have also seen evident in these chapters, the presence of these eremitic forms is indicative of some of the ways church tradition and history has developed as a result of the eremitic impulse. Moreover, the fact that the Roman Catholic worldview is situated in, and so contributes directly to, a larger Christian worldview suggests not only that the eremitic life and practice are recognized as legitimate in these contexts, but also how such recognition occurs. Again, as we have seen, many persons of religious and secular worldviews as well as of Christian and non-Christian religious traditions, seek the wisdom and insight of these Roman Catholic hermits. That is to say, through forms of hospitality, exercised in person and through a broad range of published materials as well as through print and visual media, the Roman Catholic hermit bears witness to a way of being a human person. Finally, the fact that the eremitic life is a means of approaching and embracing the universal existential call to solitude confronted by all persons indicates further both how and why the position or status of the eremitic life by fellow practitioners as well as by non-practitioners is not only recognized but embraced as a legitimate response.

Our consideration of some of the forms of eremitic life and practice in American Catholicism today is evidence for this interpretation of solitude. As we have seen, solitude has a defined place and a viable role in the American Catholic Church today. Among the variety of forms it assumes, and in its various contexts (whether of an ancient monastic order, a religious institute, or connected to the local church and diocesan bishop), the eremitic vocation to solitude is a testament to a life of undivided focus centered in contemplation in the presence of the divine. The solitude of the Roman Catholic hermit contributes to the role of eremitic life and practice in the American Catholic, and worldwide church, community. According to the 1996 post-synodal apostolic exhortation, *Vita Consecrata* (Consecrated Life), Roman Catholic hermits "bear witness to the passing nature of the present age by their inward and outward separation from the world."[14] Here, the purpose and practice of the eremitic life and practice are expressed in terms of a stable role in the present, a role that entails bearing witness by means of the cultivation of a particular form of separation; as a result, both the role and the practice of eremitic life are tied to its broader influence in the Christian and global communities. This influence, as a form of

---

14. Pope John Paul II, *Vita Consecrata* 7.

testimony, requires a particular social location defined qualitatively by the hermit's "inward and outward separation from the world." Such separation, as a form of *anachoresis* or withdrawal, is both a state, and a way, of being; it contributes to the formation of a worldview that is grounded in a form of non-attachment to the world in order to center one's life and practice on the divine presence. An insider perspective is provided by a Carthusian monk and hermit writing in *The Eremitic Life*: "The inner transformation that accompanies the hermit on his journey consists in his entrusting his human heart to God. That means a conscious and free participation in the process of ongoing life in the widest sense. So the complete response to the eremitic calling, with its character of free self-giving and sacrifice, is at the same time a profound inner protest against the degrading and lethal tumult of modern materialism. The path of eremitic discipline, besides all its other aims and meanings, is also to be a particular sign of protest, which awakens the world to the conscious and free existence deserving to be called human."[15] At the heart of the hermit's transformation as described here in these terms is an experience of solitude that is entirely individual; on some fundamental level, it is an experience that cannot be understood by appeal to language alone. This description externalizes solitude, and so provides a way of naming stages in the process of transformation. However, while the transformative experience of eremitic solitude is a highly individualized one, the exterior framework of the worldview in which solitude occurs is more broadly accessible. The transformative experience of eremitic solitude is contextualized by a community that publically supports, validates, and interprets it as such. Thus, it is possible to consider how other elements of a worldview serve to provide a structural framework for this experience. Doing so allows us an opportunity to look across various forms of eremitic life and practice considered in previous chapters in a way that draws attention to those rituals, narratives and ethical practices that unite and define these forms individually and communally. Eremitic space is a site of transformation for the hermit. Some consideration of those words and acts that define the eremitic space and locate a place for the hermit to exercise a particular way of being and of seeing the world and one's place in it serves as a site for such consideration. Given this, we may apply those dimensions of a worldview that may help to frame briefly a way of thinking about how the experience of eremitic solitude that contributes to the formation of personal eremitic identity in this space.

15. Wencel, *Eremitic Life*, 55.

Framing a Worldview in Solitude

Constructing Eremitic Space and Place

Solitude is a defining element of the eremitic life and practice considered in the previous chapters of this book. In these contexts, solitude has been defined by several distinguishing features. Consideration of some of these features will provide a way of thinking about the construction of eremitic space and place in the context of this worldview. As we have seen, one prominent feature of eremitic solitude that has been demonstrated in the forms we have considered is connected to the idea of physical withdrawal from the world. In the literature of and about the ancient desert fathers and mothers of the late fourth century, the term *anachoresis* was often used for this form of physical separation from others. In this context, physical withdrawal is an intentional act of removal for the purpose of eremitic solitude; it is a religious act, as the hermit is called to "leave the world" in order to dwell in space that is qualitatively different. This is shared by the forms examined in previous chapters. It is also enhanced by the forms considered as we have seen that physical withdrawal has an element of permanence that is guarded and defined by those guiding documents to which the hermit adheres; physical withdrawal is not undertaken for a temporary period. As well, physical withdrawal is preserved by faithfulness to promises and vows, and it is upheld by limitations on the frequency and nature of contact with the world.

The hermit's withdrawal from society is an explicit separation. In a literal sense, withdrawal is indicative of a decision to live apart and separate from others; in a symbolic sense, withdrawal demonstrates a renunciation of, or a break from, a way of being in the world. As a result, the hermit's withdrawal creates the possibility for a form of non-attachment to the world. Neither detachment not disregard, the non-attachment of the hermit is characterized by a deep sensitivity and awareness of the world, by a connection to the world through solidarity in prayer and worship. In this way, non-attachment has the effect of re-orienting the hermit to the world, and to others. This process of re-orientation will be discussed in more detail in the next section of this chapter. At this point, we want to draw attention to the fact that, for the hermit, re-orientation occurs in a particular location; eremitic withdrawal is a removal from one space for the purpose of dwelling in another space. As we have seen, eremitic space is often linked to geography ripe with religious symbolism: the space of the cave, of the woods, of the mountain, of the desert, of the valley. In the context of a religious worldview, and of a distinctively Roman Catholic worldview, such topographical features are sites of encounter and presence. It is in these areas that solitude becomes an essential, initial act in the formation of space in which the hermit can dwell in the presence of the divine. In this way, solitude is a foundational marker for the construction of eremitic space.

The structural framework of eremitic space is contextualized by those particular locations in which it is found. As we have seen, close attention is given to the natural landscape and environment in the construction of space; as scholars have observed, these offer important theological and symbolic considerations in the framing of eremitic space.[16] Architectural design of the monastery, hermitage, and cell is intentionally directed toward contemplation. This entails attention to the specific location of the eremitic site, to its design, and to its distance from others. So, for example, the Carthusian charterhouse in the United States is located on Mount Equinox; the mountain location embodies the withdrawal to be realized. Similarly, the laura of the Hermits of Bethlehem, like many contemporary lauras around the world, is found in an open area, removed from outsiders and to keep the hermits in proximity with one another. The separate dwellings in Camaldolese eremitic space retain the heightened emphasis on solitude and contemplation. Cistercian space, with its balance of communal and individual periods of work and prayer, blanketed by silence, is designed to facilitate a proper ordering of each element.

For the hermit, the experience of solitude is a means of heightening recognition of one's contingency and dependence on the divine in the context of constructed eremitic space. In order to make this less abstract, it may help to appeal to a concrete example. Consider how the significance of eremitic space as set apart and defined by solitude is articulated clearly in the following autobiographical reflection. In a candid moment during the documentary film, *Trappist*, about the Cistercian community at Mepkin Abbey in South Carolina, Abbot Francis Kline remarks: "All I need I find in this place."[17] Set apart and self-contained, the abbot indicates how space marks a Christian identity rooted in the call to solitude. As the abbot's words reveal, this identity is grounded in a sense of place. The abbot's statement of self-disclosure brings to mind what David Brown refers to in his study of space as "a wrestling with the question of how God's blessing

---

16. See the distinctive perspectives and approaches of Brown, *God and Enchantment of Place*, and of Smith, *To Take Place*, as well as Blum, "Retrieving Phenomenology of Religion," 1025–48.

17. *Trappist*. Written and directed by Robert G. Maier. Produced by John Geaney. Vision Video, 2008. DVD, 56 minutes.

will be realized within the specificity of place."[18] Such potential for what Brown terms sacramentality, by which he means, "God's communication through the material aspects of his own creation,"[19] is at the heart of the abbot's observation and can serve as the broader context in which space and place are located and defined by many of those living the eremitic life considered in this study.

The eremitic spaces examined here are bounded by the specific purpose of contemplation; the eremitic space is contemplative space characterized by acts of silence and listening. Contemplative space is intended to mark the potential for encounter. Here, too, what David Brown writes about religious geography may be considered applicable: "Taking place seriously, therefore, must mean conceding that places too, like words, can have independent revelatory power despite all the ambiguities both share."[20] As contemplative space, eremitic space offers the potential for participation in acts of prayer and worship that serve not only to recapitulate the past but to do so in a way that makes the past part of the immediate present. The eremitic spaces considered in this study are founded upon and framed by this desire.[21] Through further separation and withdrawal the hermit seeks to cultivate greater solitude; this appears as a qualitatively distinct vocation. This vocation is embodied through the cultivation of ritual practice. The regular, daily practices of prayer and worship, of work and sacred reading, of meals and rest, form a patterned rhythm which, over time, is embodied; these rituals form a life of ritual, regardless of whether the eremitic space is structured by a rule or a plan of life. One of the relevant effects of ritual in this context is the way that it structures space and time. As we have seen, the eremitic space is contemplative space; time is reflected in this contemplative space not in hours or minutes, not in days or years, but in

---

18. Brown, *God and Enchantment of Place*, 156.
19. Ibid., 245.
20. Ibid., 161.
21. On this, see Thurston, *To Everything a Season*, 10, whose reflections on time in the Christian tradition as a useful framework for thinking about this sentiment in the context of the development of eremitic practice in the United States. Thurston's work draws remarkable clarity to the distinctive conception of time in the tradition and she observes that "time is of crucial importance to a religion that claims to be historical. Christianity views time in terms of salvation history . . . For Christians, history is not a random series of events, but part of the eternal plan of Good to reconcile humanity to the Divine Life . . . *Time, in short, is the locus of God's activity.*"

the immediate presence of the self before the divine.[22] The ritual practices heighten this construction of time as they make immanent and ever present that the hermit dwells always and at all times in and before the divine presence. In solitude, in the presence of the divine, the eremitic space is a space of offering and of sacrifice wherein the hermit offers the self to be healed and transformed.[23] In these, and in many other ways, eremitic space is embodied with action, gesture and ritual; the sacred time of the liturgy and of the divine office, and sacred practices of prayer and worship, as continuous, are ways of marking the distinctiveness of the eremitic space.

As contemplative, ritualized space, eremitic space is framed by those guidelines that govern and direct the specific form of eremitic life and practice. In this way, eremitic space is narrative space; those myths and doctrines, located in sacred scripture and tradition, are embodied by the hermit in eremitic space. As narrative space, then, eremitic space provides adherence and connection to a mythic past, a historical lineage of those whose practice and wisdom, whose words and deeds, are carried into the present in the life and practice of the hermit. References to the founders, to the desert fathers and mothers of late antiquity, and to biblical figures in the rules, plans, and guiding documents of these hermits supply not only examples of the past but a lineage for the present. We have referred in previous chapters to these guidelines. Each of the forms presented here contains clear guidelines for eremitic practice. Furthermore, foundational documents in each form presented contain explicit teachings that frame the specific form. The *Camaldolese Constitutions and Declarations*, the *Constitutions of the Congregation of the Camaldolese Hermits of Monte Corona* (2002), the *Carthusian Statutes*, the *Constitutions of the Monks* (2005) of the Order of Cistercians of the Strict Observance, and the *Plan of Life of the Hermits of Bethlehem* all contain statements articulating the conditions for eremitic space. In each case, there are a few common elements. While there is restricted access in eremitic space, it is not isolationist; there are clearly articulated and espoused connections between the hermit and the community. As narrative space, eremitic space is shaped by careful consideration of the choice and use of words, by attention to the qualitative and quantitative tone of verbal expression, by the words of sacred scripture, by the words of prayer and worship, by the words of the liturgy. The words contained in the eremitic space as narrative space are centered on contemplation and ritual.

22. For a broader perspective on the relationship of space, place and otherness in religion see Davies, *Emotion, Identity, and Religion*.
23. See Chidester and Linenthal, *American Sacred Space*, 9.

Framing a Worldview in Solitude

As contemplative, ritual, narrative space, eremitic space is, furthermore, desert space. The eremitic space is simultaneously self-contained by the individual hermit and connected to others by prayer and solidarity; in some cases, it is connected by extensions of hospitality and other forms of charity. The eremitic space is simultaneously natural, as the site of ordered relations between human and divine, and constructed, as a site that is created by those practices that serve to define and perpetuate the rendering of those relations.[24] Defined by these features, eremitic space orients the hermit in a particular way.

Cultivating an Eremitic Orientation

The structural frameworks of eremitic space and of location provide an orientation to the world that the outside observer might also consider. This orientation may, again, be situated in the context of the place of the hermit in the context of the Roman Catholic worldview. Here, the eremitic worldview provides a distinct orientation to the past, to the present, and to the future. The linguistic framework for discussion of the eremitic life and practice in the present, evident in the respective organizational and foundational documents of each of the forms presented here as well as in post-conciliar documents addressing this form, emphasizes a vital role in the life of the Church and the world. This role is situated and contextualized in a historical framework that hearkens to early biblical predecessors, the example of the desert fathers and mothers, and the charisms of the founders and reformers. As a result, the hermit and the eremitic life and practice are located in a historical tradition whose roots and place are firmly established. This lineage extends into the future as others are called to cultivate the eremitic life and practice. This threefold orientation of the eremitic life and practice, orientation to the present, to the past, and to the future, may be examined separately although it appears to operate simultaneously.

In his article "The Contemplative Self," Charles Asher writes that: "The contemplative self, or moment, is a point of view. It is to view with attention. It is concentrated focus . . . It does not deny the world. It attends to the world as it is given from moment to moment."[25] Asher's insight emphasizes the heightened sensitivity and abiding awareness of the contemplative

---

24. See Lefebvre, *Production of Space*, 137, where he writes of those spaces "devoted to encounter and gratification."

25. Asher, "Contemplative Self," 31.

hermit. This description could apply, as well, to the contemplative emphasis of the eremitic life and practice. Attentive to others in solidarity and in prayer, the hermit is a listening presence in the world and before the divine. As we have seen, the solitude that is cultivated by the hermit is a solitude that is contextualized by the Catholic worldview; as a means of bearing witness, it is a solitude that is replete with intention and imitation.[26] That is to say, it is also a solitude that is defined and located in, and through, the community of the Church. Centered in the cell or hermitage, the hermit is linked through solidarity and prayer to the members of the local and global Church. Appeal to the function of the hermit, as articulated in the *Constitutions of the Monks of Montecorona*, supplies a focused statement: "Material solitude does not impede but rather reinforces mysteriously the spiritual presence of the solitary in the community of believers. If the hermit prays, it is the Church that prays in him. In the measure in which he is a living member of the Church, he fulfills perfectly the 'duty of his universality' (St. Peter Damian, Opusc. 11, 10)."[27] The relationship between the hermit and the Church suggested here indicates a shared vision and common mission that resides in the present moment; again, as a prayerful presence, the hermit bears witness in an intentional and necessary way in the current life of the local and global Church.

The eremitic orientation to the present is an orientation that is rooted in a life of contemplation. It is a life attentive to the abiding presence of the divine in and through all of creation; it is a life attentive to the deep need of human beings to be known and to be loved. The eremitic life and practice recognizes in an acutely tangible way, human failing and weakness, through sinfulness. It embodies that element of Christian life that calls all Christians to combat sin and temptation, evil and despair. Exercise of specific virtues and values in the context of solitude retains an element of separation that, in turn, permits a means of articulating an alternative course of action and responding to the needs of the church and world. The eremitic life and practice, structured as it is in this way, is a counter-cultural presence in the world today. The current rise in secularism, individualism, and materialism

---

26. Imitation is not a static practice. See Carthusian monk, *Wound of Love*, 127, which reads in reference to Jesus Christ: "And it is awesome to discover that he came to bear witness: that is, to confront each of us with a responsibility that he has to assume personally, in the depths of his own conscience."

27. *Constitutions of the Congregation of the Camaldolese Hermits of Montecorona* (2002), preface, 3. This statement, while specific to the Camaldolese Hermits of Monte Corona, may be more broadly applied to the other eremitic forms presented in this book.

shaping American society is divorced from the eremitic life and practice. The hermit stands apart and against this way of seeing and of being in the world by bearing witness to an alternative. Void of private property and ownership, not tied to material goods, or to an identity shaped by society or by professional standards, the Catholic hermits in this study espouse a worldview structured by distinct conceptions of space, place and time. Adherence to the evangelical counsels and vows grounded in the cultivation of simplicity, humility and charity, eremitic life and practice appears to decry dependence on an identity shaped by societal norms and standards. Separation and solitude provide a prophetic witness to a life that gives testimony to Jesus Christ as savior and redeemer of humankind.

Current hermits, like their ancient predecessors, are drawn into the desert to cultivate contemplation; in this way, hermits in the Roman Catholic Church are contributing to a historical tradition. Their forms of eremitic life and practice are deeply rooted in this historical tradition. The eremitic life and practice is grounded in a historical tradition of desert spirituality that draws on biblical precedents and texts, in the desert fathers and, in some cases, the founders. Explicit references to these figures are a means of associating the eremitic life and practice of the present in the framework of this historical tradition. The desert and wilderness experiences of biblical predecessors situate the eremitic life and practice in the context of scripture.[28] The charisms of those founders like St. Benedict, St. Romuald, St. Bruno, and Robert of Molesme revived and grounded anew the eremitic impulse in the monastic contexts of their day. The eremitic orientation to the past is an orientation rooted in a deep recognition of salvation history, and the particular place of those figures and events that might serve as examples and models for imitation. At the center of the eremitic offering of the self is Jesus Christ.

By bearing witness to the past through a living act of memory in the present the eremitic life and practice indicates a way of being not only in the present but a proposal for a way of being in the future. The eremitic orientation toward the future, an orientation that looks forward, that is eschatological, is an orientation filled with hope and lasting peace. It is an orientation that moves beyond the immediate, present needs of the world and towards the future. The hermit is perceived by many as a symbolic

---

28. Gruen, *Heaven Begins with You*, 18. See also Dreuille, *Seeking the Absolute Love*, 35: "The spirituality of the desert admitted of several contradictory positions, a sign of the tensions already existing in monastic life."

witness to others; the public interpretation of this witness contributes to the broader eschatological vision of the Church. This observation may apply as well to some extent to the prayerful witness of the hermit in the future as the Church continues to name and uphold a place for eremitic life and practice.

Contributing to a Vibrant Spiritual Tradition

One wonders how eremitic space and place will continue to be defined and interpreted in the context of the American Catholic Church in the future. It is certainly the case that a significant contribution has been made to the place of a desert spiritual tradition; perhaps this is a contribution that will continue to be shaped over time as participation and exposure to eremitic life and practice are maintained.

It is difficult to argue against a sustained need for the silent, prayerful witness provided by eremitic life and practice. Although the numbers of Catholics in the United States who live as hermits is small, recognition of their presence indicates that it is valued by many. One feature of this recognition is that it appears to come from a wide range of persons and segments of American society; in this sense, there is an interest that transcends the parameters of those members of the local diocese or geographic region.

By continuing to bear witness as others have done in the past, contemplative hermits in the American Catholic Church in the present are contributing to a living tradition of desert spirituality. While the current modes of interpretation are occurring in contexts spatially and temporally distinct from the past, there are several shared features. Through the inclusion of sustained, defining elements of solitude and of contemplation, and through the preservation and continuance of distinguishing root rituals of prayer and worship located in sacred scripture, eremitic life and practice is interpreted by those in the tradition as a form of desert spiritual tradition that has a place today. In this way, current forms of eremitic life and practice are important aspects of the broader foundation of contemplative life in the American Catholic Church; the eremitic life and practice, thus, stands alongside other forms of contemplative life and practice. The eremitic impulse and spirit are embedded in the Roman Catholic worldview. Cultivated in a range of practices and forms, so too is contemplation. The eremitic impulse as a contemplative one is a longstanding feature of a Roman Catholic worldview. Those forms of eremitic life and practice explored in previous chapters contribute to the wide range and variety of contemplative life in the daily life of the Roman Catholic Church in the United States and throughout the world. The desert spirituality of contemplation is an integral component of a Roman Catholic worldview. Contemplation is readily present in the liturgical practices and calendar of the Church; it is also evident in a range of temporary and permanent structural forms cultivated by monastic and lay Catholics. Ascetic disciplines are further elements of contemplative life cultivated by monastic and non-monastic Roman Catholics. In these, and in many other ways, the construction of desert space—in the world or in the human heart—is one of the many ways Roman Catholics locate a site of encounter, in which to know and define human purpose and meaning. The desert, whether literally or symbolically understood, is a means of locating that site as a place in which to dwell in order to negotiate and navigate self-identity in the context of an American Catholic worldview. In all cases, such negotiation is situated in this religious context and, as such, contributes to a broader social identity. Eremitic space and place operate and are contextualized in relationship not only to the divine, but in relationship to other human beings; connected to other monastics, to the Roman Catholic church community in a unique way through location (solitude) and through position (bearing witness), the hermit participates united with others in the life of the church.

7

Conclusion

> The hermit's whole life is a life of silent adoration. His very solitude keeps him ever in the presence of God.... His whole day, in the silence of his cell, or his garden looking out upon the forest, is a prolonged Communion.[1]

IT IS FITTING, PERHAPS, TO CONCLUDE THIS BOOK BY APPEALING TO another passage about the eremitic life and practice. The passage that opens this chapter is taken from *The Silent Life*, by the Cistercian monk, priest and hermit, Thomas Merton. Thomas Merton entered the Cistercian Order of the Strict Observance at the Abbey of Gethsemani in Trappist, Kentucky, in 1941. After many years in the monastery, he remained drawn to a deeper life of contemplation and was granted permission, in 1965, to move into a hermitage on the grounds of the monastery. The contrast between the perspective he offers in *The Silent Life* and that in the entry titled "Hermit," from the early twentieth-century edition of the *Catholic Encyclopedia* that opened the first chapter of this book, could not be a starker one.[2] Whereas the 1910 encyclopedia entry concluded by emphasizing the near dismissal of the eremitic life and its inability to thrive in an extended way in the contemporary period, the passage from *The Silent Life* presented above highlights in a more positive tone, some of the distinctive characteristics of eremitic life and practice from one of its most prominent mid-century proponents. The contexts of the lived experience of contemplation that per-

---

1. Merton, *Silent Life*, 150. Compare the statement of these features as they appear in the operative definition of hermit that is found in a study of Italian hermits by Turina, "Vers un catholicisme 'exemplaire'?," 115–33.

2. Besse, "Hermit," 7:281.

meate Fr. Merton's words helps to situate his eremitic life and practice in a deeply religious and personal way.³ Inviting and secure, his words appear to underlie, and hearken to, a hope for the longevity of eremitic life in the Church.

An Eremitic Presence in American Catholicism

The description of the eremitic life and practice in this passage from *The Silent Life* as well as those explored in previous chapters of this book certainly reflect a changed social and religious environment in American Catholicism as well.⁴ The period from the publication of the 1910 edition of the *Catholic Encyclopedia* to that of *The Silent Life* is evidence for a growing presence of the eremitic life and practice among Catholics in the United States. The perspective of stagnancy in eremitic life and practice that marks the beginning of the twentieth century appears to have shifted slightly by the middle of the century through the rise and development of several efforts, including those of select monasteries, orders and individuals like Fr. Thomas Merton to locate and support eremitic life and practice in locations across the country. One key effort is evident in the historic move, on the part of several monastic foundations, to establish new foundations in the United States. The monastic foundations of the Camaldolese, Carthusian and Cistercian Orders included in this book are relatively recent and significant developments in the histories of these Orders.⁵ These developments

---

3. Further removed, Fr. Merton wrote extensively. Tucked away, Fr. Merton's life as a hermit actually served to position him as a voice of protest against injustices in American society. His solidarity with those working for systemic change compelled his involvement in the world. While Fr. Merton's own hybridization of contemplation and activism was novel and was perceived by some as controversial in American, Catholic, and monastic contexts at the time it did serve as an influential response to the question of American Catholic identity. There is a considerable body of literature by, and about, Fr. Thomas Merton. For writings by Merton that address specifically the eremitic life and practice, see among this body of literature: *Silent Life*; *Contemplative Prayer*; *New Seeds of Contemplation*; and *Monastic Journey*, ed. Hart. On pp. 135–43 of this book, there is a blueprint for a hermitage. See also Bochen, *Thomas Merton*. On the place of solitude in American spirituality, with some attention to the connections drawn between Thomas Merton and Thoreau, see Schmidt, *Restless Souls*, 63–100. See also France, *Hermits*, 163–91.

4. The use of the phrase American Catholicism is restricted here to Roman Catholicism in the United States.

5. Fr. Merton's desire for increased separation and solitude in the context of his monastic vocation, and his effort to live a more contemplative life through eremitic practice were shared by other Catholics interested in undertaking the eremitic life on

address a need in the American Catholic Church and mark a moment in its own historical narrative. The distinct emphasis on contemplation in these contemplative Orders would come to complement the earlier presence of others, like the Carmelites and Benedictines, as well as those in religious orders who are primarily dedicated to more visible forms of service and engagement, of ministry and preaching, such as the Franciscans and Dominicans. Although the development of new monastic and eremitic foundations for the Camaldolese, Carthusian and Cistercian Orders in the United States certainly contribute, in some sense, to a broader missionary impulse, the result of these developments is not only an expanded presence of eremitic life and practice here and around the world. Indeed, the impact of eremitic life and practice is a further result. As we have seen in the evidence of previous chapters, in each case the efforts to create a monastic or eremitic foundation required the financial, social, and prayerful support of key benefactors, and church leaders, as well as members of the local church community. Galvanized around the desire to construct space for eremitic life and practice, many constituencies were responsible for contributing the resources needed for these foundations. Moreover, the presence of these foundations, and of those men and women who were called to embrace the contemplative life and practice in them, are a significant factor in the

---

American soil during this period. The Camaldolese Benedictine monk, Thomas Matus, *Nazarena*, 63, writes: "The publication of Thomas Merton's writings in Italian had given the Camaldolese the idea that Saint Romuald's hermit ideal might have a special appeal for Americans." This idea was tested successfully with the foundation years later, by the Italian Camaldolese, of the first American Camaldolese settlement in Big Sur, CA. Around the same time, on the other side of the country, the eremitic practice of the Carthusian Order was also being established on American soil on Mount Equinox, VT. Finally, as in the case of the Cistercians at the Abbey of Gethsemani, the eremitic impulse was active within those religious orders whose charism held an eremitic spirit, like the Carmelite Order, or offered the eremitic life as a form of the monastic life, like the Order of St. Benedictine. Unlike the Camaldolese Order and the Carthusian Order, these religious orders have had a longer, more established presence in the United States. Members of these religious orders who sought a deeper commitment to the contemplative life through eremitic practice did so by making arrangements through their respective administrations. Calls for renewal from Vatican Council II provided further opportunities for members of all religious orders to review their lives and practices; in some cases, renewal was an opportunity for members to consider again the place of the eremitic life in the monastic vocation. On this, Weakland, foreword to *Survival or Prophecy?*, ed. Hart, xiii, writes: "The reemergence of hermits seemed a strange phenomenon to many in those postwar years. Merton in particular felt misunderstood whenever he mentioned his desire to live as a hermit among the Camaldolese in Europe or in a simple dwelling in the woods near the Abbey of Gethsemani."

broader mid-century contemplative impulse experienced by many in the American Catholic laity. Sustained support of these establishments is evidence that a place for this impulse is still a valued one.

In a sense, what we see in the current day is a strengthening of the presence of eremitic life and practice in the United States.[6] From the mid-twentieth century to the present, the presence of eremitic life and practice has been sustained and continued, becoming more stable and established. Increased attention on, and interest in, eremitic life and practice by the larger public has contributed to the increased visibility and prominence of eremitic life and practice. Furthermore, recent ecclesiastical and juridical recognition of the canonical or consecrated hermit has allowed for another form of eremitic life and practice to be located on the landscape of American Catholicism. In particular, Canon 603 of the *Revised Code of Canon Law* provides a juridical standing for the eremitic vocation and a framework for the Roman Catholic individual called to live as a canonical, or consecrated, hermit. The standing of the canonical hermit is situated in the context of the local diocese, and the life and practice of the canonical hermit are overseen by the diocesan bishop. As a result, individuals exercise their vocations as consecrated hermits under the guidance of a plan of life approved by the diocesan bishop. While the life and practice of these hermits is intimately situated in the context of the local church community in a way that differs from those in monastic orders or new institutes, the form of eremitic life and practice of the canonical or consecrated hermit stands alongside those forms of eremitic life and practice found in these contexts. The founding of the Hermits of Bethlehem in the Heart of Jesus is evidence of one of the ways Canon 603 is being implemented in the eremitic life and practice in the United States in the twenty first century.[7] Other forms of eremitic life

---

6. It should be noted that this strengthening in the visibility of presence does not mean that the eremitic life is void of skeptics or detractors. As Colegate, *Pelican in the Wilderness*, 240, writes: "The hermit's calling is anti-institutional. It is also ecumenical. Those in the institutional churches who approve of it say that it is at the heart of the church and not separated from it, but there are others who look on it as dangerous and potentially disorderly." Observing that misunderstanding about the vitality of the eremitic vocation remains, Hall, *Silence, Solitude, Simplicity*, 88, writes: "And those who know history will remember that times of significant growth in hermit vocations have historically been times of spiritual purification in the church, a herald of profound renewal."

7. See Bargellini, "Concluding Remarks," who calls for dialogue between established, traditional forms of practice and more recent forms. See also, afterword to Casey, *Survival or Prophecy?*, ed. Hart, 136–38.

and practice in accordance with Canon 603, under a plurality of forms, are thriving in locations across the country and around the world.[8]

Papal support and ecclesiastical consideration in the form of encyclicals, and of the post-synodal apostolic exhortation, *Vita Consecrata* (Consecrated Life) in 1996, in particular, has added attention as well as further stability and credibility to these forms of eremitic life and practice in the United States. At the heart of these documents and movements appears to rest a deep and abiding recognition of the distinctive vocation to the eremitic life, a vocation that is embodied in the lived experience of the Catholic hermit. There is an effort to explain eremitic life and practice in a way that deepens and broadens understanding of its contemplative focus and of its place in the local and global church communities.

These, and many other, local and universal efforts to continue to ground and support eremitic life and practice in the United States in the current post-conciliar environment have located ways not only to support eremitic life and practice in the present but to do so in a way that facilitates and sustains the eremitic life and practice with an eye to its ongoing development in the future. Success will be dependent on many factors, one of which is the ongoing growth and development of American Catholicism. What might it mean for these forms of eremitic life and practice, marked by their solitary, silent, prayerful witness, to retain their presence on American soil? Among the many issues to be considered in response to this question is the fact that the United States is an increasingly religiously pluralistic society.[9] In his work *Roman Catholicism in America*, published in 1999, Chester Gillis writes that "socially and politically, contemporary Catholics are more diverse and less identifiable than their predecessors. There is also an increased pluralism of belief among them religiously. And while they may not look to the church for answers to all of their questions, the culture of Catholicism is deeply embedded within them."[10] These trends appear to remain in place. According to the statistics compiled by the Pew Forum on Religion & Public Life (2007), over 51 percent of Americans identify

---

8. This is an important consideration in the broader development of eremitic life and practice. See, e.g., those who are canonical hermits and who have shared their experiences with eremitic life and practice in *Raven's Bread Hermit Ministries* by Paul and Karen Fredette, at http://www.ravensbreadministries.com. See also the information about canonical hermits found in Fredette and Fredette, *Consider the Ravens*.

9. See Chaves, *American Religion*, 16–32. Chaves' study employs data from the General Social Survey and the National Congregations Study.

10. Gillis, *Roman Catholicism in America*, 3.

religious affiliation with a Protestant denomination.[11] Nearly 34 percent identify as Catholic.[12] Furthermore, in its "Summary of Key Findings," the study shows that "while those Americans who are unaffiliated with any particular religion have seen the greatest growth in numbers as a result of changes in affiliation, Catholicism has experienced the greatest net losses as a result of affiliation changes."[13] Just slightly over 40 percent of American Catholics are between the ages of 30–49, and nearly one quarter of American Catholics are between the ages of 50–64.[14] Catholics comprise less than 50 percent of the population of those states in which the eremitic forms studied here are found.[15]

At the very least, these findings indicate an American Catholic landscape presently marked by change. Changes in religious affiliation, in religious practice, and in demographics are significant markers as American Catholics define their future. Fluctuations in population growth and the sizable presence of an aging population of American Catholic practitioners will, no doubt, impact this future as well. Questions about American Catholic identity will continue to emerge and to be shaped by societal and religious factors. Attitudes towards religious life and practice, often affected as they are by age, generational differences, family background, and geographic region will also affect the construction of the American Catholic population in the future.

It is in this context that a response to the question of the place of the eremitic life and practice in American Catholicism might be offered that seeks to neither mystify nor mythologize it. As we have seen in previous chapters, regardless of the particular form presented here, with its characteristic features of physical withdrawal for the purpose of solitude and contemplation, eremitic life and practice embodies a distinctive orientation to the past, to the present, and to the future. These features and this orientation overturn many of the core operating assumptions in American society. For this reason, eremitic life and practice are deemed counter-cultural. To some extent, this is the case. At first glance, eremitic life and practice can appear disorienting. The eremitic emphasis on withdrawal and solitude can form the basis for a charge that the eremitic life and practice are selfish or

11. See Pew Forum on Religion and Public Life, "U.S. Religious Landscape Survey."
12. Ibid.
13. Ibid., "Summary of Key Findings," para. 5.
14. See ibid., "Maps," at http://religions.pewforum.org/pdf/portrait-Catholic.pdf.
15. Ibid.

self-serving. Closer examination of the eremitic life and practice through consideration of select forms here, however, challenges this claim.[16] Both the hermit and the religious worldview in which eremitic life and practice are situated define and locate eremitic life and practice specifically and concretely by connection in and through a community. The hermit, as a member of a respective religious community, and of the community of Catholics across the country and world, is in a continual state of being that is marked by solidarity, by unity with others through worship and the Eucharist, through prayer and through prophetic witness.

And so the hermit continues to draw the attention of an American Catholic public, interested in knowing more. The reasons for this may be as many and as varied as those non-participants whose curiosity is piqued and who are interested in learning about the life and practice of the hermit. Speculation on the reasons for the recent level of interest is offered by sources both familiar, and unfamiliar, with eremitic life and practice.[17] As one Camaldolese hermit writes: "It is very possible that one of the basic reasons why the life of the desert attracts so much interest nowadays is that it is an instrument for equipping the people of today with that wise distance from themselves, as well as from the world of material things."[18] From this perspective, the life of the desert appears to suggest a practical and a symbolic response to the individualism, secularism and materialism

---

16. The issue or question of the "usefulness" of the contemplative life is addressed in many ways. See Cole and Conner, *Christian Totality*, 137–39. For eremitic perspectives, consider also the position taken in *Saint Bruno Pilgrim of the Absolute*, 10, where there is recognition of the context in which questions regarding function are raised, as such questions "are a consequence of a utilitarian and technocratic culture which is inclined to assess the importance of things and even of people in relation to their immediate 'usefulness.' The consecrated life which is a life spent in loving and serving the Lord in order to devote oneself to His Person and His Mystical Body has always been looked upon by the Church as a sign of unbounded generosity transcending all 'utilitarian' considerations (cf. *Vita Consecrata*)." See also Bunge, *Earthen Vessels*, 35, who writes, "Most people have the notion that the so-called 'active orders' are far more 'useful' than the purely 'contemplative' communities. The former, in fact, are often spared when hostile measures are taken against the Church, while the contemplative orders are suppressed with no compunction as being (socially) 'useless.'"

17. A range of sources may be considered on this. The perspective of a hermit is supplied by Hall, *Silence, Solitude, Simplicity*, 91, who writes, "The temptation in recent times has been to all but submerge the solitary in the social. Perhaps we are on the way to honoring and nurturing the life-giving integration of both aspects of our human mystery. Then indeed we would have hope of a deepened relation with God, with our own truest selves, with others, and with creation."

18. Wencel, *Eremitic Life*, 4.

current in American society and culture. Those interested in an alternative perspective, in a perspective that challenges the operating assumptions upon which principles of acquisition, private ownership, and attachment to materials goods is based, may find one in the eremitic life and practice. Some consideration of American society through this perspective may afford an opportunity for critical reflection.[19]

It is noteworthy that this tension between difference and sameness, between proximity and distance, resonates with many non-eremitic outsiders who share testimony of their experiences with those cultivating eremitic life and practice. The testimony of visitors, of retreatants, and of others, regardless of religious affiliation or worldview, who have spent time among these hermits often tell of an encounter with a form of otherness, as the eremitic focus on solitude, contemplation, and listening are recognized clearly as offering an alternative way of being, and of being a Roman Catholic, in particular, in society. For some, the opportunity to participate, albeit briefly, in desert spirituality that is rooted in the intentional construction and ordering of eremitic space facilitates a reimagining of the present. Heightened awareness of the silence that surrounds the eremitic space, of the quality of speech, of the intentionality of gesture, and of adjustment to the daily *horarium* are some of the more immediate distinctions experienced and articulated by the outsider. Outsiders notice the way that hospitality is exercised, the quality of the interactions between individuals, and the ways that time and space are ritualized. For many outsiders, it is precisely because the eremitic life and practice indicates a possible way of being, that their experiences may provide them with a way of re-orienting their own worldview; an outsider's encounter with contemplation and charity, for example, may empower the outsider to live and to bear witness in a more centered, intentional way, united with others by bonds of a shared humanity.

Eremitic life and practice are currently a vibrant presence in the American Catholic Church. In the context of this religious worldview, vibrancy is

---

19. See Bausch, *Catholics in Crisis?*, 195, who observes that, among several other things, "the beginnings of a great revival of our mystical tradition along with the development of an everyday spirituality to meet the very palatable hunger for God so evident today." With regard to the role of monastic and eremitic life and practice, in particular, we should also note that it is likely that access to information will continue to be impacted by technological advancement, and changes in forms of communication; decisions about websites and about email communication, for example, are among those items to be addressed. Print media, in the form of books, newsletters, and articles will be affected as well. See Rourke, *Social and Political Thought of Benedict XVI*, 85–86.

not gauged by numbers of adherents or practitioners, nor is it the product of an outwardly visible religiosity. It is not the result of testimonials expressing the impact and influence of eremitic life and practice. Rather, the current vibrancy of eremitic life and practice is due to its solid foundation in the Roman Catholic worldview. The eremitic life and practice is grounded in solitude, silence and listening; it is a life shaped by work, prayer, and ascetic discipline; it is a life of faith, hope, and charity. Its vibrancy is determined and defined not quantitatively, but qualitatively, as eremitic life and practice is a contemplative presence in the American Catholic Church. Measured not by the exterior standards of success and failure operative in American society, its future rests on the sustained support for, and cultivation of, the interior standards and contemplative life it seeks to maintain.

An Eremitic Witness in American Catholicism

During the eleventh and twelfth centuries, monastic reformers gave close attention to the eremitic life.[20] The increase of eremitic practice, evident in the lives of St. Romuald of Ravenna, Robert of Molesme, and St. Bruno of Cologne, represented a stress on the individual spiritual journey undertaken in the context of the Christian monastic community. The emphasis these men placed on austerity, simplicity, poverty and obedience underlie a return to that dimension of the Christian life characterized by the single-minded focus on the solitary struggle. The vision of eremitic life espoused by these men, and by those reformers who would come in some cases to shape generations to follow, as it would be embedded in the Camaldolese, Cistercian, and Carthusian Orders, respectively. Their contributions to desert spirituality offered a response to the contemporary churches of their day that recalled and redefined the contemplative life in the eremitic practice.

Centuries later, as we have seen, the eremitic life can still be realized as a viable form of practice in these Orders. The guiding documents of these Orders contain teachings that address spiritual, practical and administrative considerations connected to the eremitic life and practice. The teachings in these documents do not stand alone; in each case, a long tradition of eremitic life and practice can be found. This tradition illustrates another longstanding feature, namely, the fundamental definition of the eremitic life and practice as a lived worldview, connected to others in the order, in the church, and in the world. The call to reflection and renewal issued by

20. See Leyser, *Hermits and the New Monasticism*.

Vatican Council II, and accepted by the members of these religious orders, further qualifies the place of the eremitic life and practice. Clearly, eremitic life and practice remain a fundamental, defining element in these Orders today. Each Order retains a space and a place for the hermit, and for the eremitic life, that assures a connection to those communities that nurture and sustain it.

Canonical recognition of the consecrated hermit is a significant development with regard to eremitic life and practice in the Roman Catholic Church. Specifically, the content of Canon 603 in the *Revised Code of Canon Law* provides an opportunity and a structure for those called to a particular form of eremitic life and practice in a diocesan context. The forms of eremitic life and practice to be designated under Canon 603 are determined by the hermit and ecclesiastical authority. These parties work together to decide the specific form that the eremitic life and practice will assume. Location of life and practice, plan of life, and elements of spiritual guidance, for example, are jointly decided. In the context of the local church community, consecrated hermits can live the form of eremitic life to which they are called.

There are several common features among the forms of eremitic life and practice that have been presented and considered in this book. Physical withdrawal to a removed or remote site facilitates the construction of an eremitic space that is structured by solitude. Solitude and silence are distinguishing features of the contemplative life and practice undertaken in the eremitic space. Ritual practices and ascetic disciplines facilitate the development of eremitic space. These practices and disciplines render distinct constructions of place and of time. Heightened attentiveness to acts of speaking and hearing, grounded in the cultivation of silence and listening, orients the hermit to past, present, and future. Awareness of place renders acts of hospitality and charity that unite the hermit to those in the community, Church and world. The vibrant contemplative presence of the hermit in the United States is evidence of a particular way of being a Roman Catholic. There is no indication that the need for this presence will decrease; perhaps, if anything, the need for this presence will increase. Regardless of need, however, the question of whether the eremitic life and practice is sustainable in American Catholicism is an important one. In the context of a diverse, religiously pluralistic society, and despite increased public interest and media attention, the eremitic life and presence is still largely a silent presence on American soil. As a result, for many, this presence remains not

Conclusion

only a realized one but a symbolic one, as the American Catholic hermit continues to bear witness in a contemplative life of solitude and in silence before all.

Bibliography

Abbass, Jobe. *The Consecrated Life: A Comparative Commentary of the Eastern and Latin Code.* Ottawa: Faculty of Canon Law, Saint Paul University, 2008.

Abbot, Walter M., ed. *The Documents of Vatican Council II.* New York: America, 1996.

Allchin, A. M., ed. *Solitude and Communion: Papers on the Hermit Life Given at St. David's, Wales in the Autumn of 1975.* Oxford: SLG, 1977.

Aprile, Dianne. *The Abbey of Gethsemani: Place of Peace and Paradox; 150 Years in the Life of America's Oldest Trappist Monastery.* Stratford, ON: Trout Lily, 1998.

Asher, Charles. "The Contemplative Self." In *Depth Psychology: Meditations in the Field,* edited by Dennis Patrick Slattery and Lionel Corbett, 22–32. Einsiedeln, Switzerland: Daimon, 2000.

Bamberger, John Eudes. "Fragments for a Vision of Cistercian Life in the 21st Century." In *A Monastic Vision for the 21st Century: Where Do We Go From Here?,* edited by Patrick Hart, 119–44. Kalamazoo, MI: Cistercian, 2006.

———. "Spiritual Accompaniment: Observing Love and Its Transformations." *Cistercian Studies Quarterly* 37 (2002) 415–19.

Barbour, John D. *The Value of Solitude: The Ethics and Spirituality of Aloneness in Autobiography.* Charlottesville: University of Virginia Press, 2004.

Bargellini, Emanuelle. "Concluding Remarks: Camaldoli's Recent Journey and Its Prospects." In *The Privilege of Love: Camaldolese Benedictine Spirituality,* edited by Peter-Damian Belisle, 183–88. Collegeville: Liturgical, 2002.

Barnhart, Bruno. "Monastic Wisdom: The Western Tradition." In *The Privilege of Love: Camaldolese Benedictine Spirituality,* edited by Peter-Damian Belisle, 61–80. Collegeville: Liturgical, 2002.

Bausch, William J. *Catholics in Crisis? The Church Confronts Contemporary Challenges.* Mystic, CT: Twenty-Third, 1999.

Beal, John P., et al., eds. *New Commentary on the Code of Canon Law.* Study Ed. Mahwah, NJ: Paulist, 2000.

Belisle, Peter-Damian. *Camaldolese Spirituality.* Bloomingdale, OH: Ercam, 2007.

———. "The 'Hermit' Archetype within the Monastic Spiritual Journey." *Word & Spirit* 15 (1993) 41–50.

———. *The Language of Silence: The Changing Face of Monastic Solitude.* Maryknoll: Orbis, 2003.

———. "Overview of Camaldolese History and Spirituality." In *The Privilege of Love: Camaldolese Benedictine Spirituality,* edited by Peter-Damian Belisle, 3–28. Collegeville: Liturgical, 2002.

———. "Primitive Romualdian/Camaldolese Spirituality." *Cistercian Studies Quarterly* 31 (1996) 413–29.

———, ed. *The Privilege of Love: Camaldolese Benedictine Spirituality.* Collegeville: Liturgical, 2002.

Bell, Daniel. *Liberation Theology after the End of History.* New York: Routledge, 2001.

Bibliography

Bell, David N. "Is There Such a Thing as 'Cistercian Spirituality'?" *Cistercian Studies Quarterly* 33 (1998) 455–72.

———. *Understanding Rancé: The Spirituality of the Abbot of La Trappe in Context.* Kalamazoo, MI: Cistercian, 2005.

Bellitto, Christopher M. *Renewing Christianity: A History of Church Reform from Day One to Vatican II.* New York: Paulist, 2001.

Berman, Constance H. *Medieval Agriculture, the Southern French Countryside, and the Early Cistercians: A Study of Forty-Three Monasteries.* Philadelphia: American Philosophical Society, 1986.

———, trans. *Women and Monasticism in Medieval Europe: Sisters and Patrons of the Cistercian Reform.* Selected by Constance H. Berman. Kalamazoo, MI: Medieval Institute, 2002.

Besse, Jean. "Hermit." In *Catholic Encyclopedia*, 7:281. New York: Robert Appleton, 1910.

Beyer, Jean. *The Law of Consecrated Life: Commentary on Canons 573–606.* Paris: Tardy, 1988.

Bianco, Frank. *Voices of Silence: Lives of the Trappists Today.* New York: Anchor, 1991.

Blum, Jason N. "Retrieving Phenomenology of Religion as a Method for Religious Studies." *Journal of the American Academy of Religion* 80 (2012) 1025–48.

Bokenkotter, Thomas. *A Concise History of the Catholic Church.* Rev. and expanded ed. New York: Image, 1990.

Bondi, Roberta. *To Love as God Loves: Conversations with the Early Church.* Philadelphia: Fortress, 1987.

Boyle, Joseph. "Cistercian Grace Today: Conformity to Christ." *Cistercian Studies Quarterly* 35 (2000) 279–82.

Breck, John. "Prayer of the Heart: Sacrament of the Presence of God." In *The Contemplative Path: Reflections on Recovering a Lost Tradition*, edited by E. Rozanne Elder, 39–64. Kalamazoo, MI: Cistercian, 1995.

Brown, David. *God and the Enchantment of Place.* New York: Oxford University Press, 2004.

Brown, Peter. *The Cult of the Saints: Its Rise and Function in Latin Christianity.* Chicago: University of Chicago Press, 1981.

———. *Power and Persuasion in Late Antiquity: Towards a Christian Empire.* Madison: University of Wisconsin Press, 1992.

Bunge, Gabriel. *Earthen Vessels: The Practice of Personal Prayer according to the Patristic Tradition.* Translated by Michael J. Miller. San Francisco: Ignatius, 2002.

Burns, Robert A. *Roman Catholicism after Vatican II.* Washington, DC: Georgetown University Press, 2001.

Burton-Christie, Douglas. *The Word in the Desert: Scripture and the Quest for Holiness in Early Christian Monasticism.* New York: Oxford University Press, 1993.

Butler, Cuthbert. *Benedictine Monachism.* 1924. Reprint, Eugene, OR: Wipf & Stock, 2005.

Camaldolese hermit [anon.]. *In Praise of Hiddenness: The Spirituality of the Camaldolese Hermits of Monte Corona.* Edited by Louis-Albert Lassus. Bloomingdale, OH: Ercam, 2007.

The Canon Law Letter & Spirit: A Practical Guide to the Code of Canon Law. Prepared by the Canon Law Society of Great Britain and Ireland. Collegeville: Liturgical, 1995.

Bibliography

Caparros, Ernest, et al., eds. *Code of Canon Law Annotated*. Montreal: Wilson & Lafleur, 1993.
Carthusian monk [anon.]. *Carthusian Saints*. Arlington, VT: Charterhouse of the Transfiguration, 2006.
Carthusian monk [anon.]. *The Freedom of Obedience: Carthusian Novice Conferences*. Translated by an Anglican solitary [anon.]. Kalamazoo, MI: Cistercian, 1998.
Carthusian monk [anon.]. *Poor therefore Rich: Carthusian Novice Conferences*. Translated by an Anglican solitary [anon.]. Kalamazoo, MI: Cistercian, 1999.
Carthusian monk [anon.]. *The Prayer of Love and Silence*. Translated by a monk of Parkminster [anon.]. Kalamazoo, MI: Cistercian, 1998.
Carthusian monk [anon.]. *They Speak by Silences*. Translated by a monk of Parkminster [anon.]. Kalamazoo, MI: Cistercian, 1996.
Carthusian monk [anon.]. *The Wound of Love: A Cathusian Miscellany*. Herefordshire, UK: Gracewing, 2006.
Carthusian retreatant [anon.]. "Carthusian Life and Its Inner Spirit." Arlington, VT: Charterhouse of the Transfiguration, 2005. Originally written ca. 1950.
"Carthusians in America: The Foundation." Charterhouse of the Transfiguration. http://transfiguration.chartreux.org/Foundation.htm.
Casey, Michael. "Thoughts on Monasticism's Possible Futures." In *A Monastic Vision for the 21st Century: Where Do We Go from Here?*, edited by Patrick Hart, 23–42. Kalamazoo, MI: Cistercian, 2006.
Chaves, Mark. *American Religion: Contemporary Trends*. Princeton: Princeton University Press, 2011.
Chidester, David, and Edward T. Linenthal. *American Sacred Space*. Bloomington: Indiana University Press, 1995.
Chryssavgis, John. "Fire and Light in the Egyptian Desert: Aspects of Desert Spirituality." *Cistercian Studies Quarterly* 34 (1999) 455–67.
Cobb, Richard. *Times Literary Supplement*, 25 December 1981, 1483.
Cody, Aelred. "The New Canons on Consecrated Life and the Mind of the Council." In *The Revised Code of Canon Law: A Missed Opportunity*, edited by Peter Huizing and Knut Walf, 64–68. Edinburgh: T. & T. Clark, 1981.
Cole, Basil, and Paul Conner. *Christian Totality: Theology of the Consecrated Life*. Revised and updated, incorporating the papal exhortation *Vita Consecrata*. New York: Alba House, 1997.
Colegate, Isabel. *A Pelican in the Wilderness: Hermits, Solitaries and Recluses*. Washington, DC: Counterpoint, 2002.
Collins, Mary. *Contemplative Participation: Sacrosanctum Concilium Twenty-Five Years Later*. Collegeville: Liturgical, 1990.
Conchuir, Alphonsus O. "Diminishing Communities." *Cistercian Studies* 14 (1979) 135–44.
Conley, John J. "The Eremitical Anthropology of William of St. Thierry." *Cistercian Studies* 25 (1990) 115–30.
Consiglio, Cyprian. "An Image of the Praying Church: Camaldolese Liturgical Spirituality." In *The Privilege of Love: Camaldolese Benedictine Spirituality*, edited by Peter-Damian Belisle, 29–46. Collegeville: Liturgical, 2002.
The Constitutions of the Congregation of the Camaldolese Hermits of Monte Corona. Bloomington, OH: Camaldolese Congregation of the Order of Saint Benedict, 2002. http://camaldolese.org/pdfs/constitution.pdf.

Bibliography

The Constitutions and Declarations to the Rule of Saint Benedict. Translated by Thomas Matus. Bloomington, OH: Camaldolese Congregation of the Order of Saint Benedict, 2000. http://www.catholiclawyersmalaysia.org/sites/default/files/constitutions_of_the_benedictines.pdf.

Constitutions of the Monks (2005). Order of Cistercians of the Strict Observance, 2005. http://www.ocso.org/index.php?option=com_docman&Itemid=122&lang=en.

Cook, John W., and Allan Doig. "Architecture." In *Encyclopedia of Christianity*, edited by John Bowden, 59. Oxford: Oxford University Press, 2005.

Corcoran, Donald. "A Wild Bird, with God in the Center: The Hermit in Community." In *The Privilege of Love: Camaldolese Benedictine Spirituality*, edited by Peter-Damian Belisle, 145–55. Collegeville: Liturgical, 2002.

Coriden, James A., et al., eds. *The Code of Canon Law: A Text and Commentary.* New York: Paulist, 1985.

Council of Major Superiors of Women Religious. *The Foundations of Religious Life: Revisiting the Vision.* Notre Dame: Ave Maria, 2009.

Cross, Robert D. *The Emergence of Liberal Catholicism in America.* Cambridge: Harvard University Press, 1967.

Cunningham, Lawrence S. *The Catholic Heritage: Martyrs, Ascetics, Pilgrims, Warriors, Mystics, Theologians, Artists, Humanists, Activists, Outsiders, and Saints.* New York: Crossroad, 1983.

Customs of the Congregation of the Camaldolese Hermits of Montecorona and the Ceremonial for the Divine Office. Bloomington, OH, 2009. http://www.camaldolese.org/customary2009.doc.

Dahari, Uzi. *Monastic Settlements in South Sinai in the Byzantine Period: The Archeological Remains.* Jerusalem: Israel Antiquities Authority, 2000.

Dardenne, Myriam. "The Christian Contemplative Community." *Cistercian Studies* 3 (1968) 328–36.

Davies, Douglas J. *Emotion, Identity, and Religion: Hope, Reciprocity, and Otherness.* New York: Oxford University Press, 2011.

Dimier, Anselme. *Stones Laid before the Lord: A History of Monastic Architecture.* Translated by Gilchrist Lavigne. Kalamazoo, MI: Cistercian, 1999.

Dolan, Jay P. *The American Catholic Experience: A History from Colonial Times to the Present.* Notre Dame: University of Notre Dame Press, 1992.

Donkin, R. A. *The Cistercians: Studies in the Geography of Medieval England and Wales.* Toronto: Pontifical Institute of Medieval Studies, 1978.

Downey, Michael. *Trappist: Living in the Land of Desire.* Mahwah, NJ: Paulist, 1997.

Dreuille, Mayeul de. *Seeking the Absolute Love: The Founders of Christian Monasticism.* New York: Crossroad, 1999.

Dubois, Gérard. "Authority and Obedience in Contemporary Monasticism." Translated by James Jarzembowski. *Cistercian Studies* 8 (1973) 101–8.

Dubois, Marie-Gérard. "The Order of Cistercians of the Strict Observance." *Cistercian Studies* 16 (1981) 182–93.

Dulles, Avery. *The Reshaping of Catholicism: Current Challenges in the Theology of Church.* San Francisco: Harper & Row, 1988.

"Early Times: The Sixties." Transcribed and edited from the "Early Times" section of the Equinox Mountain website. Charterhouse of the Transfiguration. http://transfiguration.chartreux.org/Early-Times.htm.

Bibliography

Ebaugh, Helen Rose Fuchs. *Women in the Vanishing Cloister: Organizational Decline in Catholic Religious Orders in the United States*. New Brunswick: Rutgers University Press, 1993.

Edwards, Tudor. *Worlds Apart: A Journey to the Great Living Monasteries of Europe*. New York: Coward-McCann, 1958.

Elder, E. Rozanne, ed. *The New Monastery: Texts and Studies on the Early Cistercians*. Kalamazoo, MI: Cistercian, 1998.

Emery, Kent, Jr., and *Analecta Cartusiana*. *The Charterhouse of the Transfiguration: Two Historical Essays*. Arlington, VT: Charterhouse of the Transfiguration (2009), 1–6.

Evans, Gillian Rosemary. *Bernard of Clairvaux: Selected Works*. Mahwah, NJ: Paulist, 1987.

Farkasfalvy, Denis. "Biblical Vocabulary as a Reflection of the Spirituality of the Founders of Citeaux." In *The New Monastery: Texts and Studies on the Early Cistercians*, edited by E. Rozanne Elder, 156–57. Kalamazoo, MI: Cistercian, 1998.

Fergusson, Peter. "Cistercian Architecture." In *A Companion to Medieval Art: Romanesque and Gothic in Northern Europe*, edited by Conrad Rudolph, 577–98. Malden, MA: Blackwell, 2006.

Fitzpatrick, Gail. "Enclosure: The Heart of the Matter." In *A Monastic Vision for the 21st Century*, edited by Patrick Hart, 145–64. Kalamazoo, MI: Cistercian, 2006.

Fogarty, Gerald P. "North America." In *Modern Catholicism: Vatican II and After*, edited by Adrian Hastings, 326–33. London: Oxford University Press, 1991.

Fracchia, Charles A. *Living Together Alone: The New American Monasticism*. San Francisco: Harper & Row, 1979.

France, Peter. *Hermits: The Insights of Solitude*. New York: St. Martin's, 1996.

Fredette, Paul A., and Karen Karper Fredette. *Consider the Ravens: On Contemporary Hermit Life*. Bloomington, IN: iUniverse, 2008.

Freeman, Brendan. *Come and See: The Monastic Way for Today*. Kalamazoo, MI: Cistercian, 2010.

Fry, Timothy, trans. *The Rule of St. Benedict*. New York: Random House, 1998.

Gaillardetz, Richard R., and Catherine E. Clifford. *Keys to the Council: Unlocking the Teaching of Vatican II*. Collegeville: Liturgical, 2012.

Garraghan, Gilbert J. "The Trappists of Monks Mound." In *Chapters in Frontier History: Research Studies in the Making of the West*, 94–135. Milwaukee: Bruce, 1934.

Gerosa, Libero. *Canon Law*. New York: Continuum, 2002.

Gillis, Chester. *Roman Catholicism in America*. New York: Columbia University Press, 1999.

Gould, Graham. *The Desert Fathers on Monastic Community*. Oxford: Clarendon, 1993.

Gran, John Willem. *A Hand on My Shoulder*. 2 vols. Kalamazoo, MI: Cistercian, 2004.

Green, Thomas J. "The Revised Code of Canon Law: Some Theological Issues." *Theological Studies* 47 (1986) 617–52.

Gruen, Anselm. *Heaven Begins with You: Wisdom from the Desert Fathers*. New York: Crossroad, 1999.

Guigo. *The Solitary Life*. A letter of Guigo, 5th prior of the Grande Chartreuse. Translated by Thomas Merton. Arlington, VT: Charterhouse of the Transfiguration, 2006. http://transfiguration.chartreux.org/Guigo-Letter-Solitude.htm.

Hale, Robert. "*Koinonia*: The Privilege of Love." In *The Privilege of Love: Camaldolese Benedictine Spirituality*, edited by Peter-Damian Belisle, 99–114. Collegeville: Liturgical, 2002.

Bibliography

———. *Love on the Mountain: The Chronicle Journal of a Camaldolese Monk.* Trabuco Canyon, CA: Source, 1999.

Hall, Jeremy. *Silence, Solitude, Simplicity: A Hermit's Love Affair with a Noisy, Crowded, and Complicated World.* Collegeville: Liturgical, 2007.

Halpern, Sue. *Migrations to Solitude.* New York: Pantheon, 1992.

Hardon, John A. *Catechism on Consecrated Life.* Bardstown, KY: Eternal Life, 2000.

Hart, Patrick, ed. *A Monastic Vision for the 21st Century: Where Do We Go From Here?* Kalamazoo, MI: Cistercian, 2006.

———. *Survival or Prophecy? The Correspondence of Jean Leclercq and Thomas Merton.* Kalamazoo, MI: Cistercian, 2008.

———. *Thomas Merton, Monk: A Monastic Tribute.* Kalamazoo, MI: Cistercian, 1983.

Hartt, Frederick. *History of Italian Renaissance Art: Painting, Sculpture, Architecture.* New York: Abrams, 1979.

Hastings, Adrian. "St. Benedict and the Eremitical Life." *Downside Review* 68 (1950) 191–211.

"Hermit." In *Oxford Dictionary of the Christian Church*, edited by F. L. Cross, 766. 3rd rev. ed., edited by Elizabeth A. Livingstone. Oxford: Oxford University Press, 2005.

Heyer, Kristin E. *Prophetic & Public: The Social Witness of U. S. Catholicism.* Washington, DC: Georgetown University Press, 2006.

Hirschfeld, Yizhar. *The Judean Desert Monasteries in the Byzantine Period.* New Haven: Yale University Press, 1992.

Hite, Jordan, et al., eds. *A Handbook on Canons 573–746.* Collegeville: Liturgical, 1985.

Hoguet, Robert Louis. *Robert Louis Hoguet (1878–1961): An Autobiography.* New York: Vantage, 1986.

Hutchison, Carole A. *The Hermit Monks of Grandmont.* Kalamazoo, MI: Cistercian, 1989.

Inge, John. *A Christian Theology of Place.* Aldershot, UK: Ashgate, 2003.

Into Great Silence. Film. Directed by Philip Gröning. United Kingdom: Zeitgeist, 2006.

Isherwood, Lisa. "Embodying and Emboldening Our Desires." In *Interpreting the Postmodern: Responses to "Radical Orthodoxy,"* edited by Rosemary Radford Ruether and Marion Grau, 161–74. New York: T. & T. Clark, 2006.

Jasper, David. *The Sacred Desert: Religion, Literature, Art, and Culture.* Malden, MA: Blackwell, 2004.

Johnson, Bernard. "The Charter of Charity and the New Constitutions." *Cistercian Studies* 2 (1967) 221–35.

Keller, David G. R. *Oasis of Wisdom: The Worlds of the Desert Fathers and Mothers.* Collegeville: Liturgical, 2005.

Kiser, John W. *The Monks of Tibhirine: Faith, Love, and Terror in Algeria.* New York: St. Griffin, 2002.

Kline, Francis. "To What Holiness? Monasticism and the Church Today." In *A Monastic Vision for the 21st Century*, edited by Patrick Hart, 165–84. Kalamazoo, MI: Cistercian, 2006.

Knowles, David. *Christian Monasticism.* New York: McGraw-Hill, 1969.

———. *From Pachomius to Ignatius: A Study in the Constitutional History of the Religious Orders; The Sarum Lectures 1964–65.* Oxford: Clarendon, 1966.

Koch, Philip. *Solitude: A Philosophical Encounter.* Chicago: Open Court, 1994.

Komonchak, Joseph A. "Towards a Theology of the Local Church." FABC Papers, presented at the FABC Theological Advisory committee meeting, April 4–14, 1986, 1–43.

Bibliography

Krailsheimer, A. J. *Rancé and the Trappist Legacy*. Kalamazoo, MI: Cistercian, 1985.
Lawler, Philip F. "Silence and Solitude: Unchanged in 900 years." *Catholic World Report* (2001) 50–55. Reprinted in *Silence and Solitude*. Arlington, VT: Charterhouse of the Transfiguration (2005), 9–19.
Leclercq, Jean. *Alone with God*. New York: Farrar, Straus & Cudahy, 1961.
———. *The Love of Learning and the Desire for God: A Study of Monastic Culture*. New York: Fordham University Press, 1982.
Leclercq, Jean, and Paul Giustiniani. *Camaldolese Extraordinary: The Life, Doctrine, and Rule of Blessed Paul Giustiniani*. Edited by the Camaldolese Hermits of Monte Corona. Bloomington, OH: Ercam, 2003.
Lefebvre, Henri. *The Production of Space*. Translated by Donald Nicholson-Smith. Oxford: Blackwell, 1991.
Lekai, Louis J. *The Cistercians: Ideals and Reality*. Kent, OH: Kent State University Press, 2000.
———. *The Rise of the Cistercian Strict Observance in Seventeenth Century France*. Washington, DC: Catholic University of America Press, 1968.
Lentfoehr, Thérèse. "The Solitary." In *Thomas Merton, Monk: A Monastic Tribute*, edited by Patrick Hart, 59–78. Kalamazoo, MI: Cistercian, 1983.
Leyser, Henrietta. *Hermits and the New Monasticism: A Study of Religious Communities in Western Europe, 1000–1150*. New York: St. Martin's, 1984.
Lillich, Meredith Parsons, ed. *Studies in Cistercian Art and Architecture*. Vol. 4. Kalamazoo, MI: Cistercian, 1993.
Lockhart, Robin Bruce. *Halfway to Heaven: The Hidden Life of the Carthusians*. Kalamazoo, MI: Cistercian, 1985 & 1999.
Louf, André. "The Apostolic and Contemplative Dimension of Religious Life." *Cistercian Studies* 22 (1987) 111–25.
———. *The Cistercian Way*. Kalamazoo, MI: Cistercian, 1989.
———. "Living in Community." *Cistercian Studies* 21 (1986) 81–95.
———. "Solitudo Pluralis." In *Solitude and Communion: Papers on the Hermit Life*, edited by A. M. Allchin, 17–29. Oxford: SLG, 1977.
———. *The Way of Humility*. Translated by Lawrence S. Cunningham. Kalamazoo, MI: Cistercian, 2007.
Louf, André, et al. "Contemplatives and the Crisis of Faith." 1967. Available in an English in Thomas Merton, *The Monastic Journey*, edited and translated by Patrick Hart, 174–78. Kalamazoo, MI: Cistercian, 1992.
MacDonald, Helen L. "Hermits: The Juridical Implications of Canon 603." *Studia canonica* 26 (1992) 163–89.
Maguire, Nancy Klein. *An Infinity of Little Hours: Five Young Men and Their Trial of Faith in the Western World's Most Austere Monastic Order*. New York: Public Affairs, 2006.
Martin, Dennis D., trans. *Carthusian Spirituality: The Writings of Hugh of Balma and Guigo de Ponte*. Mahwah, NJ: Paulist, 1997.
Martin, Francis. "Cistercian Monasticism and Modern Adaptations." *Cistercian Studies* 3 (1968) 281–327.
Martin, Thomas F. *Our Restless Heart: The Augustinian Tradition*. Maryknoll: Orbis, 2003.
Massa, Mark S. *The American Catholic Revolution: How the '60s Changed the Church Forever*. New York: Oxford University Press, 2010.

Bibliography

Matus, Thomas. *The Mystery of Romuald and the Five Brothers: Stories from the Benedictines and Camaldolese*. Trabuco Canyon, CA: Source, 1996.

———. *Nazarena: An American Anchoress*. New York: Paulist, 1998.

Matus, Thomas, and Salvatore Frigerio. *The Monastic Life of the Camaldolese Benedictines*. Trabuco Canyon, CA: Source, 1994.

Matus, Thomas, and Robert Hale. "Camaldolese in Dialogue: Ecumenical and Interfaith Themes in the History of the Camaldolese Benedictines." In *The Privilege of Love: Camaldolese Benedictine Spirituality*, edited by Peter-Damian Belisle, 157–68. Collegeville: Liturgical, 2002.

McBrien, Richard P. *Catholicism: Study Edition*. New York: Harper & Row, 1981.

McDermott, Rose. "Recent Developments on Issues of Religious Law." *Bulletin on Issues of Religious Law* 9 (1993) 1–9.

McGinn, Bernard. "Ocean and Desert as Symbols of Mystical Absorption in the Christian Tradition." *Journal of Religion* (1994) 155–81.

Merton, Thomas. *Contemplation in a World of Action*. Garden City, NY: Doubleday, 1971.

———. *Contemplative Prayer*. New York: Image, 1971.

———. "A Letter on Solitude and Community." Edited by Patrick Hart. *Cistercian Studies* 25 (1990) 75–78.

———. *The Monastic Journey*. Edited by Patrick Hart. Kalamazoo, MI: Cistercian, 1992.

———. *New Seeds of Contemplation*. New York: New Directions, 1972.

———. *Pre-Benedictine Monasticism: Initiation into the Monastic Tradition 2*. Edited by Patrick F. O'Connell. Kalamazoo, MI: Cistercian, 2006.

———. *The Rule of Saint Benedict: Initiation into the Monastic Tradition 4*. Edited by Patrick F. O'Connell. Kalamazoo, MI: Cistercian, 2009.

———. *The Seven Storey Mountain*. Orlando: Harcourt, 1998.

———. *The Silent Life*. Canada: HarperCollins, 1996.

———. *The Silent Life of the Carthusians*. Modern version excerpted from Merton's classic text. Originally published by Farrar, Straus & Giroux, 1957. Arlington, VT: Charterhouse of the Transfiguration, 2009. http://transfiguration.chartreux.org/Merton-on-Carthusians.htm.

———. *Thomas Merton: Essential Writings*. Selected by Christine M. Bochen. Modern Spiritual Masters. Maryknoll: Orbis, 2000.

Monk [anon.]. *The Hermitage Within: Spirituality of the Desert*. Translated by Alan Neame. London: Darton, Longman & Todd, 1999.

Mutrux, Robert H. *Architecture of Contemplation*. Arlington, VT: Charterhouse of the Transfiguration, 2005. Originally published in *Great New England Churches*. Globe Pequot, 1982.

———. *Great New England Churches*. Chester, CT: Globe Pequot, 1982.

Nash, David J. "Deserts." In *Patterned Ground: Entanglements of Nature and Culture*, edited by Stephan Harrison et al., 153–56. London: Reaktion, 2004.

Neenan, Benedict. *Thomas Verner Moore: Psychiatrist, Educator and Monk*. Mahwah, NJ: Paulist, 2000.

Negev, Avraham, and Shimon Gibson, eds. *Archaeological Encyclopedia of the Holy Land*. Rev. ed. New York: Continuum, 2001.

Nigg, Walter. *Warriors of God*. New York: Knopf, 1959.

Nouwen, Henri J. M. *The Genessee Diary: Report from a Trappist Monastery*. New York: Doubleday, 1981.

Bibliography

Novices of Mont-des-Cats. "The Grace and Law of Silence." *Cistercian Studies* 3 (1968) 187–88.

O'Brien, David J. *The Renewel of American Catholicism*. New York: Paulist, 1972.

O'Connor, Cronan. *New Melleray Abbey: Trappist Life in 20th Century America*. Photos by Lawrence Nolan. Dubuque, IA: New Melleray Abbey, 1967.

Olivera, Bernardo. "A Monastic Vision for the 21st Century." In *A Monastic Vision for the 21st Century: Where Do We Go From Here?*, edited by Patrick Hart, xiii–xvii. Kalamazoo, MI: Cistercian, 2006.

O'Neal, Laurel M. "Eremitism: Call to the Chronically Ill and Disabled." *Review for Religious* (1989) 234–39.

Pease, William J. "Out of Great Silence: A Carthusian Interlude." *Commonweal*, February 29, 2008. https://www.commonwealmagazine.org/out-great-silence-0.

Perata, David. *The Orchards of Perseverance: Conversations with Trappist Monks about God, Their Lives, and the World*. Ruthven, IA: St. Therese's, 2000.

Pew Forum on Religion and Public Life. "U.S. Religious Landscape Survey." February 2008. http://religions.pewforum.org/maps.

Phipps, Colin. "Romuald Model Hermit: Eremitical Theory in Saint Peter Damian's Vita Beati Romualdi, Chapters 16–27." In *Monks, Hermits and the Ascetic Tradition*, edited by W. J. Sheils, 65–77. Oxford: Blackwell, 1985.

Pini, Virginia. "The Order of Cistercians of the Strict Observance." *Cistercian Studies* 16 (1981) 194–200.

Pohl, Christine D. *Making Room: Recovering Hospitality as a Christian Tradition*. Grand Rapids: Eerdmans, 1999.

Pollard, Miriam, and Thomas X. Davis. "Monastic Solitude according to Our Cistercian Tradition." *Cistercian Studies Quarterly* 40 (2005) 411–21.

Pope John Paul II. *Captivated by Him Who Is Only Love*. Message of Pope John Paul II for the ninth centenary of Saint Bruno's death. Arlington, VT: Charterhouse of the Transfiguration, 2006. Appeared in *L'Osservatore Romano*, English weekly ed. 24, June 13, 2001, 6–7.

———. "God Alone Is the Source of True Peace." Message of Pope John Paul II on his visit to the town and charterhouse of Serra San Bruno, Italy, October 5, 1984. Arlington, VT: Charterhouse of the Transfiguration, 2011.

———. *Vita Consecrata*. Post-synodal apostolic exhortation. Issued March 25, 1996.

Pope Paul VI. *Ecclesiae Sanctae*. Apostolic letter, written Motu Proprio, on the implementation of the Decrees Christus Dominus, Presbyterorum Ordinis and Perfectae Caritatis. Issued August 6, 1966. http://www.papalencyclicals.net/Paul06/p6ecclss.htm.

Pope Pius XI. *Contemplatives in the Heart of the Church: The Solemn Teaching of Pope Pius XI on the Apostolic Value of Carthusian Life*. Arlington, VT: Charterhouse of the Transfiguration, 2006.

Power, David N. *Gifts That Differ: Lay Ministries Established and Unestablished*. New York: Pueblo, 1985.

Raymond, M. *Burnt Out Incense: The Saga of Citeaux American Epoch*. New York: Kennedy, 1949.

Regular Life: Monastic, Canonical, and Mendicant Rules. 2nd ed. Selected and introduced by Daniel Marcel La Corte and Douglas J. McMillan. Kalamazoo, MI: Medieval Institute, 2004.

Rippinger, Joel. *The Benedictine Order in the United States: An Interpretive History*. Collegeville: Liturgical, 1990.

Bibliography

Robinson, David. "A Journey through Monastic Prayer." *St. Antony Messenger*, January 2011, 22–23.

Romano, Eugene L. *In the Silence of Solitude: Contemporary Witnesses of the Desert.* New York: Alba House, 1995.

———. *A Way of Desert Spirituality: The Plan of Life of the Hermits of Bethlehem.* Rev. ed. New York: Alba House, 1998.

Rorimer, James J. *The Cloisters: The Building and the Collection of Mediaeval Art.* New York: Metropolitan Museum of Art, 1951.

Rourke, Thomas R. *The Social and Political Thought of Benedict XVI.* Lanham, MD: Lexington, 2011.

Russell, Kenneth. "The Dangers of Solitude." *Review for Religious* (2000) 575–83.

———. "Must Hermits Work?" *Review for Religious* (2000) 159–74.

Saint Bruno as Seen by His Contemporaries. Selection of contributions to Saint Bruno's funeral parchment. Translated by a Carthusian monk [anon.]. Arlington, VT: Charterhouse of the Transfiguration, 2009.

Saint Bruno Pilgrim of the Absolute. Collection of reflections by various Carthusians on Saint Bruno. 4 vols. Arlington, VT: Charterhouse of the Transfiguration, 2011.

Saint Bruno. *Two Letters and the Profession of Faith.* Arlington, VT: Charterhouse of the Transfiguration, 2005.

"St. Romuald." In *Oxford Dictionary of the Christian Church*, edited by F. L. Cross, 1426. 3rd rev. ed., edited by Elizabeth A. Livingstone. Oxford: Oxford University Press, 2005.

Sayre, Robert. *Solitude in Society: A Sociological Study in French Literature.* Cambridge: Harvard University Press, 1978.

Schaefer, Jean Owens. "The Earliest Churches of the Cistercian Order." In *The New Monastery: Texts and Studies on the Early Cistercians*, edited by E. Rozanne Elder, 1–12. Kalamazoo, MI: Cistercian, 1998.

Schlegel, Gerhard, and James Hogg, eds. *Monasticon Cartusiense.* Vol. 4, pt. 2. Salzburg, 2006. Reprinted in *The Charterhouse of the Transfiguration: Two Historical Essays.* Arlington, VT: Charterhouse of the Transfiguration (2009), 7–15.

Schmidt, Leigh Eric. *Restless Souls: The Making of American Spirituality.* San Francisco: HarperSanFrancisco, 2005.

Schneiders, Sandra M. *Religious Life in a New Millennium.* Vol. 1, *Finding the Treasure: Locating Catholic Religious Life in a New Ecclesial and Cultural Context.* Mahwah, NJ: Paulist, 2000.

Sciascia, Giuseppina. *The Silent Summer of 1944: Carthusian Monks in Italy Opened Their Doors, Saving Many from Death Camps.* Arlington, VT: Charterhouse of the Transfiguration, 2006. Appeared first in *L'Osservatore Romano*, English weekly ed. 24, February 2, 2005, 4–5.

Serratelli, Arthur. "Consecrated Life: Icon of the Church, Icon of God." *Beacon.* News of the Diocese of Paterson. http://www.patersondiocese.org.

Sheils, W. J., ed. *Monks, Hermits and the Ascetic Tradition: Papers Read at the 1984 Summer Meeting and the 1985 Winter Meeting of the Ecclesiastical History Society.* Oxford: Blackwell, 1985.

Skudlarek, William. *Demythologizing Celibacy: Practical Wisdom from Christian and Buddhist Monasticism.* Collegeville: Liturgical, 2008.

Smart, Ninian. *Worldviews: Crosscultural Explorations of Human Beliefs.* 2nd ed. Englewood Cliffs, NJ: Prentice Hall, 1995.

Bibliography

Smith, Huston. *Why Religion Matters: The Fate of the Human Spirit in an Age of Disbelief.* SanFrancisco: Harper, 2001.

Smith, Jonathan Z. *To Take Place: Toward Theory in Ritual.* Chicago: University of Chicago Press, 1987.

Smith, Tom. "A Day in the Life of the Monks of Historic Gethsemani." *St. Louis Post-Dispatch*, December 24, 1989.

Spencer, Jeffry, and Michael Fish. "The Camaldolese Oblate Program: History, Tradition, Charism." In *The Privilege of Love: Camaldolese Benedictine Spirituality*, edited by Peter-Damian Belisle, 169–82. Collegeville: Liturgical, 2002.

Spreafico, Rosaria. "The Community, Subject of Evangelization (I)." *Cistercian Studies Quarterly* 41 (2006) 351–68.

Statutes of the Carthusian Order. Excerpts from books 1–9. http://transfiguration.chartreux.org/Texts.htm.

Stewart, Columba. *Prayer and Community: The Benedictine Tradition.* Maryknoll: Orbis, 1998.

Steyn, Carol. "The Charterhouse of Nonenque: A Discussion of an Existing Medieval Nunnery in the Context of Carthusian Architecture." *South African Journal of Art History* 21 (2006) 1–20.

Storr, Anthony. *Solitude: A Return to the Self.* New York: Free Press, 1988.

Sweeney, Jon M. *Cloister Talks: Learning From My Friends the Monks.* Grand Rapids: Brazos, 2009.

Teahan, John F. "Solitude: A Central Motif in Thomas Merton's Life and Writings." *Journal of the American Academy of Religion* 50 (1982) 521–38.

Thurston, Bonnie. *To Everything a Season: A Spirituality of Time.* Eugene, OR: Wipf & Stock, 1999.

Trappist. Written and directed by Robert G. Maier. Produced by John Geaney. Vision Video, 2008. DVD, 56 mins.

Truyen, Vincent. "Are Monks Religious?" *Cistercian Studies* 2 (1967) 236–42.

Tsafrir, Yoram, ed. *Ancient Churches Revealed.* Jerusalem: Israel Exploration Society, 1993.

Turina, Isacco. "Vers un catholicisme 'exemplaire'?" *Archives de sciences sociales des religions* 133 (2006) 115–33.

Tvedten, Benet. *The Motley Crew: Monastic Lives.* Collegeville: Liturgical, 2007.

Urban, Cori Fugere. "Carthusians Mark 900th Anniversary of Founder's Dies Natalis." *Vermont Catholic Tribune*, October 5, 2001, 11–14. Reprinted in *Silence and Solitude*. Arlington, VT: Charterhouse of the Transfiguration (2005), 1–8.

Van Wanroij, Macarius. "The Prophet Elijah Example of Solitary and Contemplative Life." *Carmelus* 16 (1969) 251–63.

Vatican Council II. *Ad Gentes.* Decree on the Church's missionary activity. Washington, DC: National Catholic Welfare Conference. In *Documents of Vatican Council II.* New York: America, 1966.

———. *Lumen Gentium.* Dogmatic constitution on the Church. November 21, 1964. Washington, DC: National Catholic Welfare Conference. In *Documents of Vatican Council II.* New York: America, 1966.

———. *Perfectae Caritatis.* Decree on the appropriate renewal of the religious life. Washington, DC: National Catholic Welfare Conference. In *Documents of Vatican Council II.* New York: America, 1966.

Vigilucci, Lino. *Camaldoli: A Journey into Its History and Spirituality.* Translated by Peter-Damian Belisle. Trabuco Canyon, CA: Source, 1995.

Bibliography

Vina. Produced and directed by Philip Garvin. Religious America series. Boston: WGBH, 1973.Videocassette (VHS), 27:44.

Vogüé, Adalbert de. "The Rule of Saint Benedict and the Contemplative Life." *Cistercian Studies* 1 (1966) 54–73.

———. "Saint Benedict and Spiritual Progress: The Author of the Rule between His Source and His Biographer." *Cistercian Studies Quarterly* 34 (1999) 279–98.

Voth, M. Agnes. *Green Olive Branch*. Chicago: Franciscan Herald, 1973.

Ward, Benedicta. "The Relationship between Hermits and Communities in the West with Special Reference to the Twelfth Century." In *Solitude and Communion: Papers on the Hermit Life*, edited by A. M. Allchin, 22. Oxford: SLG, 1977.

Weigel, George. *Witness to Hope: The Biography of Pope John Paul II*. New York: HarperCollins, 1999.

Weil, Dean C. "Religion Journal: A Monastery Uniting the Old and New." *New York Times*, January 12, 2002, 16.

Weisenbeck, Marlene. *The Vocation to Eremitic Life*. A guidebook on the formation process for the Eremitic life. LaCrosse, WI: Office of Consecrated Life, 1997.

Wencel, Cornelius. *The Eremitic Life: Encountering God in Silence and Solitude*. Bloomingdale, OH: Ercam, 2007.

White, Carolinne, trans. *The Rule of St. Benedict*. New York: Penguin, 2008.

Williams, David H. "The Early Cistercian Documents: What Have They to Say to Us Today?" *Cistercian Studies Quarterly* 34 (1990) 299–310.

Williams, Rowan. *Where God Happens: Discovering Christ in One Another*. Boston: New Seeds, 2005.

Wilkins, Agnes. "On Hermits and Pilgrim Monks: Some Reflections on the Rule of St. Benedict, Ch. 1." *Cistercian Studies Quarterly* 16 (1981) 213–20.

Wojcik, Michael. "Holy Ground: Bethlehem Hermitage in Chester Marks 30th Anniversary." *Beacon*. News of the Diocese of Paterson. http://www.patersondiocese.org/page.cfm?Web_ID=1424.

Wong, Joseph. "The Threefold Good: Romualdian Charism and Monastic Tradition." In *The Privilege of Love: Camaldolese Benedictine Spirituality*, edited by Peter-Damian Belisle, 81–99. Collegeville: Liturgical, 2002.

Workman, Herbert B. *The Evolution of the Monastic Ideal, from the Earliest Times Down to the Coming of the Friars: A Second Chapter in the History of Christian Renunciation*. Boston: Beacon, 1962.

Zarnecki, George. *The Monastic Achievement*. New York: McGraw-Hill, 1972.

www.ingramcontent.com/pod-product-compliance
Lightning Source LLC
Chambersburg PA
CBHW051110160426
43193CB00010B/1387